MAGGIE BEER'S SPRING HARVEST RECIPES brings together over 80 of Maggie's signature springtime recipes, detailed descriptions of her favourite ingredients and inspiring accounts of memorable meals with family and friends.

The recipes highlight Maggie's philosophy of using the freshest and best seasonal produce available in the Barossa Valley, South Australia, and treating it simply, allowing the natural flavours to speak for themselves. Describing herself as a 'country cook', Maggie cooks from the heart and is passionate about instilling in others this same confidence – to use recipes as a starting point, and be guided by instinct and personal taste.

This collection of recipes from one of Australia's best-loved cooks has been taken from *Maggie's Harvest* and is essential for anyone with an appreciation of the pleasures of sourcing, cooking and sharing food.

✦ ✦ ✦

MAGGIE BEER is one of Australia's best-known food personalities. As well as appearing as a guest chef on *MasterChef Australia* and writing books, Maggie devotes her time to her export kitchen in the Barossa Valley, which produces a wide range of pantry items for domestic and international markets. These include her famous verjuice, pâté and quince pastes, her ice cream as well as her sparkling non-alcoholic grape drinks. Maggie was also recognised as Senior Australian of the Year in 2010 for inspiring joy to many Australians through food.

Maggie is the author of many successful cookbooks, *Maggie's Christmas*, *Maggie Beer* (Lantern Cookery Classics), *Maggie's Verjuice Cookbook*, *Maggie's Kitchen*, *Maggie's Harvest*, *Maggie's Table*, *Cooking with Verjuice*, *Maggie's Orchard* and *Maggie's Farm*, and co-author of the bestselling *Stephanie Alexander and Maggie Beer's Tuscan Cookbook*.

maggiebeer.com.au

MAGGIE BEER'S
SPRING HARVEST
– RECIPES –

Maggie Beer

with photography by Mark Chew

LANTERN

an imprint of
PENGUIN BOOKS

For Colin

CONTENTS

INTRODUCTION

MY PASSION FOR FOOD HAS GIVEN ME SO MUCH IN LIFE — a sense of purpose, a delicious anticipation of each new day, and gifts of a much deeper kind than financial. Harvesting the bounty from living off the land, sharing the harvest with my family and friends, and being part of a community are incredibly rewarding — I wouldn't swap my life for anything!

Maggie's Harvest, a landmark book when it was first published in 2007, was the culmination of a lot of hard work and highlights my philosophy of using the freshest and best seasonal produce available at my doorstop in the Barossa Valley. And while the original *Harvest* edition still lives in its beautifully bound embroidered cover, for ease of use, what better way to approach each season than with a paperback edition, featuring exclusively the recipes you'll need for the months ahead? More practical in the kitchen — although you need to know how much I love to see splattered copies of any of my books — this paperback, along with the rest in the series, celebrate my love for each season and bounty it brings, accentuating the produce available.

Spring is all about new life. And springtime in the garden is the most exciting time of all. The first signal that spring is coming to the farm is the almond tree slowly blossoming, while it is still cold.

In our orchard, when spring finally arrives there is a sea of apricot blossoms, then waves of plum, apple and pear blossoms, never all together but gradually filling the trees with flowers. The garden comes alive with sage, thyme and rosemary in a purple-flowered profusion. And French tarragon tendrils push back up through the earth after having lain dormant through winter.

But it is the asparagus patch that is a marvel to watch; one day nothing but a bed of straw and then suddenly the heads push through. Those first few asparagus don't usually make it to the pot — they're often eaten straight from the garden.

I hope you'll enjoy the recipes for this most magic of seasons.

ARTICHOKES

AS REVERED AS THEY ARE IN MEDITERRANEAN CUISINES, it continually surprises me how globe artichokes are so often ignored here. Many would be familiar with the pickled varieties as a tasty addition to antipasto platters and pasta dishes, but it is the fresh artichoke I long for. Our family never tire of artichoke season, often eating them straight from the garden every second day when we've had a good year. We have ten to twelve plants and replace about half of them each year, as the artichoke bears less prolifically after the first few years.

We certainly have the right climate for growing them here in South Australia, as evidenced by the large number of wild artichokes that grow as noxious weeds in the countryside and need constant digging out or spraying. The artichoke can look quite forbidding, with the tough outer leaves tightly enclosing the globe, the bristly choke that protects the heart (although sometimes the choke is edible) and the thick stem, which needs to be peeled back to its inner core. There are two main varieties sold commercially in South Australia. One has a choke that is so insignificant you can eat the whole of it early in the season. The other is larger, with a hairier choke that needs to be scraped out. If all this sounds like a lot of work, rest assured that it's well worth the effort.

Like most vegetables, the most important thing is to buy artichokes at their very freshest. If you are lucky you may be able to find a grower, such as mine in Angle Vale, who will cut them for you while you wait, or when I grow more than I need myself. If you require a large amount, for pickling for example, you can let them know your requirements ahead of time. They can be ready for you in wet hessian bags and you can spend the rest of the day pickling – the fresher, the better. The difference in flavour of the just-picked artichoke, whether for eating fresh or pickling, is huge.

The sight of a huge bouquet of artichokes on the table is a delight and, as they are so easy to grow and look quite spectacular sharing a bed with roses, this is not difficult to organise if you have the space. While some varieties of globe artichoke are actually available as early as

late May, the artichokes in our garden do not begin until mid-August, then continue to produce until the first hot weather hits. We almost binge on fresh artichokes each spring.

The traditional way to prepare artichokes is to trim the first few centimetres from the top and rub the cut surface with lemon juice or verjuice to stop discolouration. Peel off the darker outer leaves and then rub any exposed surface with the acidulant, then soak them in acidulated water until you are ready to cook them. Boil the artichokes in salted

water with a few fresh bay leaves and lemon slices added, until tender. They take about 20 minutes to cook, depending on their size. An enamelled or stainless steel saucepan is essential, as an aluminium pan will cause severe discolouration of both the artichokes and the pan.

Perhaps artichokes are something of an acquired taste and not the easiest vegetable to eat. They look so bold, so dramatic when spread out on a plate like a flower, yet few restaurateurs use them whole. Their argument is that not enough people have the confidence to tackle them and, to be sure, they do require a little knowledge to eat.

It's worth it, though; not only do artichokes have a great flavour, they are a food to become involved in – with your fingers, which are a must in this case. The simplest way is to open the artichoke up and serve it with hot butter or your chosen sauce. Pick each leaf from the outside, dip it in sauce or butter and then suck on it, leaving the fibrous remains of the leaf. When you get to the choke you can discard the hairy part. But if the artichoke is young and fresh and of the right variety, and the choke is soft instead of thorny, you can eat the lot. It can be messy – be sure to have finger bowls and plenty of napkins on the table.

I love artichokes in all forms, though if treated with disrespect and overcooked they can taste like old tea leaves. They are delicious when they have been immersed in extra virgin olive oil and braised at a low temperature. Another alternative is to cut them in quarters, squeeze lemon juice or verjuice over them and sauté them quickly in olive oil or butter for about 10 minutes.

At the end of the season baby artichokes are available. They are the lateral buds pruned from the main plant. These are the ones we preserve for use during summer as the season finishes, sometime in November. If you are not inspired to pickle your own, there are plenty of commercial artichoke hearts in oil and vinegar available bottled and loose from delicatessens. However, they will only be as good as the quality of the oil and vinegar used (and I find many of them far too vinegary), so unless you seek out imported Italian ones from artisan producers who grow and pickle their own, nothing will ever taste as good as pickling your own just-picked artichokes. Pickled artichokes have myriad uses – such as on an antipasto plate with olives, pickled lemons and prosciutto. All of these foods can be sitting in the pantry or refrigerator, perfect for a 'spur of the moment' meal requiring virtually no effort.

Preserved artichoke hearts can be used as a bed for a dish of grilled chicken livers or can be tossed with a warm salad of quail. They can also be used for an artichoke risotto, with a brandade (purée of salt cod), or simply in a salad, but be mindful of the quality of the vinegar used so its flavour doesn't dominate.

I love preserved artichokes so much that a few years ago I tried, in conjunction with the artichoke industry, to come up with some specialist artichoke products using fresh and sweet tiny artichokes. After a few unsuccessful attempts, I finally came to the conclusion that processing the artichoke immediately after picking is the only way to retain its wonderful nutty sweetness. The best-quality artichoke products I've tasted come from the small artisan growers and producers themselves.

SANTIN FAMILY PRESERVED ARTICHOKES

The Santin family, who live on the Adelaide plains, used to grow their own artichokes and preserve them, and the secret to the flavour was the freshness of the artichoke. This recipe was given to me by them just as it is here, with no specific quantities included (but to give you an idea, I would use 2 cloves of garlic to every 10 tiny artichokes). To be sure of their keeping qualities it is important to use a sterilised jar and to store the preserved artichokes in the refrigerator. This is because raw garlic used in preserves kept at room temperature can spoil. Ordinarily I would resist using garlic when preserving, only adding it if it is part of a cooked recipe, such as tomato sauce for pasta.

I now like to use verjuice instead of vinegar, and combine it with extra virgin olive oil at a ratio of 1:1. The additional oil gives another dimension, but I wouldn't recommend doing this if you use vinegar. Greatest care is required with any preserving as botulism can occur.

tiny artichokes	garlic, peeled
lemon	salt
white-wine vinegar	dash of extra virgin olive oil
flat-leaf parsley, chopped	

Take as many tiny artichokes as available and clean them by taking off the outside leaves and cutting off the top third of the globe. Rub the cut surfaces with lemon.

Put the artichokes in a stainless steel or enamelled saucepan, cover with vinegar and bring to the boil for about 5 minutes or until just tender, being careful not to overcook. Remove and dry carefully with a tea towel, then discard vinegar mixture. In a large stainless steel bowl, mix the parsley, whole garlic cloves, salt and a little olive oil and toss in the cooked artichokes. The amounts will depend on your personal taste and the number of artichokes you have. Put into sterilised jars (see Glossary) and cover completely with vinegar. They are best kept refrigerated, where they will last for a few months.

JANNI'S BRAISED ARTICHOKES WITH ARTICHOKE PURÉE *Serves 8*

One of the most memorable artichoke dishes I ever had in a restaurant was cooked by Janni Kyritsis, chef of the much-missed Sydney restaurant MG Garage. For lunch I ate a braised artichoke sitting on a bed of beautiful pale-green artichoke purée that, in turn, sat atop a crouton. The two halves of the artichoke had been deep-fried first, then braised to perfection in extra virgin olive oil with slices of carrot, slivers of garlic and flat-leaf parsley.

When I rang Janni to ask if he would share the recipe with me he said that the very next day several more people 'in the trade' had been as glowing in their praise as I was, so he decided that he would sit down there in the restaurant to eat the whole dish himself, to see what all the fuss was about. Why not try my version of it yourself?

8 thin slices toasted focaccia

good extra virgin olive oil, to serve

gremolata (chopped flat-leaf parsley, crushed
    garlic and grated lemon rind), to serve

rind of ½ lemon, finely chopped

1 teaspoon each sea salt flakes and
    freshly ground black pepper

1 cup (250 ml) white wine

BRAISED ARTICHOKES

8 large globe artichokes

juice of 1 lemon

325 ml extra virgin olive oil

1 onion, finely chopped

2 tablespoons chopped thyme leaves

2 teaspoons chopped dill

½ cup chopped flat-leaf parsley

1 carrot, thinly sliced

8 cloves garlic, thinly sliced

ARTICHOKE PURÉE

½ cup (125 ml) extra virgin olive oil

½ onion, sliced

6 artichokes (about 250 g),
    trimmed and peeled

½ clove garlic, chopped

2 teaspoons lemon juice

sea salt flakes and freshly ground
    black pepper

To make the braised artichokes, trim the artichoke stems approximately 2 cm from the bases and remove tough outer leaves, then cut in half and remove the hairy chokes from the centres. Place the artichokes in a bowl of water acidulated with the lemon juice to stop discolouration. Heat 125 ml of the olive oil in a frying pan over medium–high heat and fry artichokes lightly, then discard oil. Fry the onion in the remaining 200 ml oil, then remove from heat and stir through the chopped herbs.

Stuff the artichoke cavities and between the leaves with the onion and herb mixture. Arrange the stuffed artichokes tightly, and standing upright, in a stainless steel saucepan. Add the remaining ingredients to the pan, then cover with a sheet of baking paper and a lid. Simmer over low heat for about 20–30 minutes or until soft. Cool artichokes in their cooking juices; they are best served the next day.

To make the artichoke purée, heat the olive oil in a stainless steel saucepan, then fry the onion over low heat until soft. Add the artichokes and fry lightly without browning.

Pour in 125 ml water, then cover with baking paper and a lid and simmer over low heat for 20 minutes or until tender.

Remove artichokes, place in a blender with garlic and lemon juice, then blend, slowly adding enough of the cooking juices to make a purée. Pass through a mouli, then season to taste.

Preheat the oven to 150°C and heat the braised artichokes in their juices. Spread the hot toasted focaccia with artichoke purée. Arrange 2 artichoke halves on each slice of focaccia, then serve with extra virgin olive oil, gremolata and sea salt.

ARTICHOKES AND MUSHROOMS BRAISED IN VERJUICE AND EXTRA VIRGIN OLIVE OIL

Serves 6

This is a dish I cooked for a group of friends once when we were in France together. To make a meal of the dish I added baby onions and small waxy potatoes to the artichokes and cooked them all together.

1 cup (250 ml) verjuice
6 globe artichokes
200 ml extra virgin olive oil
8 black peppercorns, cracked
3 fresh bay leaves

2 tablespoons unsalted butter
100 g mushrooms
sea salt flakes and freshly ground black pepper
½ cup chopped flat-leaf parsley

Place the verjuice in a glass or ceramic bowl. Trim the artichoke stems approximately 2 cm from the bases and remove tough outer leaves, then cut in half and remove the hairy chokes from the centres. Place the artichokes in the verjuice to stop discolouration.

In a large, wide, stainless steel frying pan, heat 70 ml of the olive oil over medium heat. Drain the artichokes, reserving the verjuice, then pat dry with kitchen paper and quickly seal them in the pan. Cover with the remaining olive oil and reserved verjuice then add the peppercorns and bay leaves. Place a sheet of baking paper closely over the top and cook over low heat on the stove. After 45 minutes, heat the butter in a frying pan over medium–high heat and sauté the mushrooms, then season with salt and pepper. Add the mushrooms to the artichokes for the final 15 minutes of cooking.

Transfer the vegetables to a serving dish, toss with parsley, then season to taste and add a little of the cooking juices.

RAGOÛT OF GLOBE AND JERUSALEM ARTICHOKES WITH MUSHROOMS

Serves 6

This recipe marries globe artichokes with Jerusalem artichokes. They share a delicious earthy, nutty sweetness and overlap slightly in seasons.

6 Jerusalem artichokes

juice of 1 lemon

150 g butter

6 golden shallots, thinly sliced

300 g large mushrooms
   (preferably pine or cèpe) *or* large
   field mushrooms, thinly sliced

300 g shiitake mushrooms, stalks discarded
   and caps thinly sliced

6 sprigs thyme

sea salt flakes and freshly ground
   black pepper

6 small globe artichokes,
   outer leaves removed

1 lemon, halved

extra virgin olive oil, for cooking

3 teaspoons balsamic vinegar *or* vino cotto
   (see Glossary)

¼ cup chopped flat-leaf parsley

Slice the Jerusalem artichokes and place them in a bowl of water acidulated with the lemon juice to stop discolouration.

Heat 50 g of the butter in a frying pan over medium heat until nut-brown. Sauté the shallots until softened, then add the mushrooms and thyme, adding extra butter as required. Season to taste with salt and pepper, transfer to a bowl and set aside. Wipe out the pan.

Quarter the globe artichokes and remove and discard the chokes if necessary. Rub with lemon juice. Toss the globe artichokes in the clean frying pan with 50 g of the butter over medium heat until slightly golden. Transfer to the bowl with the mushrooms. Add the Jerusalem artichokes to the pan and sauté in the remaining butter with a dash of olive oil, to inhibit burning, until slightly golden. Return the mushroom and globe artichoke mixture to the pan and toss to combine. Sprinkle with balsamic vinegar or vino cotto and parsley and serve with crusty bread.

ASPARAGUS

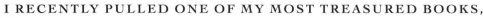 **I RECENTLY PULLED ONE OF MY MOST TREASURED BOOKS,** *The Food Lover's Garden* by Angelo Pellegrini, from the shelves and re-read: '. . . when I use the word "gardening" my reference is invariably to the cultivation of those plants, such as asparagus, that are used as food; and those, such as rosemary, that are used to make food taste good. In other words, my approach to gardening is fundamentally utilitarian. I cultivate as much of the necessary herbs, vegetables, and fruit as time and place and space will allow, in order to enjoy a fine, even a distinguished, dinner every day.'

Pellegrini inspired me when we first moved to our cottage years ago. So much so that every tree or vine we planted on our 20 acres was food-bearing, and our orchard and vegetable garden became part of our lives, no matter how busy we were. Even though many of us have work or family commitments that preclude us from being able to enjoy fine dinners from the fruits of our own labour in our kitchen garden, we can, with a few herbs, well-chosen fruits and vegetables, supply ourselves with the 'special things' that can add that touch of extravagance and freshness to our table. This is particularly true if we choose those fruit and vegetables that are more difficult or expensive to obtain.

Asparagus comes immediately to mind. You really know spring has arrived when you see asparagus on sale. Although for the first week or two it is fairly pricey, that first taste of spring is worth the extra expense. In the Pheasant Farm Restaurant days we had a great thing going with the Fanto family, who would deliver asparagus spears, picked straight from their garden, two or three times a week. Rita Fanto, who delivered them, would be insistent that we put them in a vase of water, like flowers, as they had just been cut. We were so impressed with her that she became a full-time employee, working for many years as an integral part of the pâté-making team, then moving on to the export kitchen.

At the beginning of the season, little more than thin stems are available. These used to be my favourite, but now I tend to choose the plumpest – but only if they jump out at me in

a way that only a just-picked vegetable can, with tight buds and shiny stalks. You will soon know whether you've chosen good asparagus if the stem snaps when you break it off about a third of the way up from the end. The woody bits are rejected – I don't peel the ends, an arduous task that has more to do with tradition than necessity if you've bought well. If your asparagus fails the snap test, add a pinch of sugar to the cooking water with the salt.

Asparagus crowns (the part of the plant under the soil) usually need to be at least five years old before they will start to produce a really substantial crop. Most of the ones for sale are two years old, and you will usually need to go to a grower to get them, although some nurseries do sell them – New Gippsland Seeds and Bulbs (www.newgipps.com.au) have crowns in June and seeds at other times. Perversely, however, my new asparagus patch boasts twelve two-year-old crowns that have become rampant in the six months since I planted them. I was instructed to let them get firmly established by not picking any the first spring – the aim was to encourage thicker stalks next year. The trick to harvesting your own asparagus is remembering to pick them before they shoot away to just long thin strands.

Four plants will keep a family in asparagus right through until the hot weather hits – to the point where, as there are only two of us, Colin and I can get sick of it, though we never tire of the spears we eat raw straight from the garden, and our friends are happy to take the excess. We also have a patch of wild asparagus that grows on an incline down near the chook yard, but it's very thin and straggly and can be quite bitter.

Whilst nothing quite beats freshly poached asparagus with nut-brown butter or hollandaise, particularly if it's made with verjuice (see page 12), if you have your own patch you will need some more ideas. Try a salad of asparagus, caramelised garlic cloves and pitted olives, drizzled with an extra virgin olive oil and lemon juice vinaigrette and topped with grilled goat's cheese croutons. Medium spears can be brushed with extra virgin olive oil then barbecued on a hot grillplate and served with a squeeze of lemon juice. Anxd don't forget how well asparagus goes with a traditionally smoked leg of ham.

While talking traditional, how long has it been since you enjoyed fresh white bread – thinly sliced, crusts off – spread with good butter (salted, as asparagus needs salt) and wrapped around fat, just-cooked asparagus?

Old hat, I know, but you can't go past asparagus soup – a purée of the stalks (not any woody ends, though) with the tips kept as a garnish. All you need is vegie or chicken stock to cook the chopped asparagus in, then add seasoning and a little cream, and purée. Put the blanched tips in warmed soup bowls, then pour in the soup, add some chervil and you're done.

Or perhaps poached asparagus could be added to an omelette, along with thin shavings of Taleggio cheese that melt as the omelette is turned.

When catering for a party, try poaching a mass of really fat asparagus – my favourite of all. I don't own an asparagus cooker and find no need for one – I use a wide, flat stainless steel pan with sides 5 cm high. I bring water to the boil, add salt and simmer asparagus lying flat in the pan in a single layer. Cook till done (3–4 minutes, depending on size), then drain, arrange on a large platter and immediately brush with warm butter to gloss. Present with a huge bowl of thick, luscious verjuice hollandaise to dip into – great with drinks or on a buffet table. Using verjuice in the hollandaise will give you an astounding flavour. If making a hollandaise seems like too much trouble and you're going to eat the asparagus warm, then take a good dollop of butter and heat it to the nut-brown stage in a small frying pan. Just coat the warm asparagus with that, plus sea salt and freshly ground black pepper. It is polite to eat asparagus with your fingers, so have finger bowls on the table and remember to place any hollandaise or other sauce near the tips of the asparagus rather than the stems.

Don't forget a soft-poached egg served with asparagus and shaved Parmigiano Reggiano; let the asparagus stalks be the 'soldiers' to dip into the just-cooked yolk.

White asparagus has a much more delicate flavour than green asparagus. It is grown in a similar manner to celery, with earth mounded around it like a pyramid for the whole of its growing life, and the only part to gain any colour is the tip that breaks out of the ground. This is certainly something for the home gardener to consider.

Though my preference is for green, the white is revered by many and could be used in any of the recipes given here. The best white asparagus I've had was blanched for a few minutes in boiling salted water then gently pan-fried in nut-brown butter.

While staying with Patricia Wells in Vaison-la-Romaine in Provence, we bought a bunch of white asparagus at the wonderful food market there. Patricia peeled the asparagus, then steamed the spears before quickly refreshing them in iced water. She then lightly sautéed the asparagus in oil, and served it with a squeeze of lemon. Delicious!

GRILLED ASPARAGUS WITH VERJUICE HOLLANDAISE

Serves 4 as an entrée

I like to serve asparagus with hollandaise. When I do, I begin to make the hollandaise just as I put the water for cooking the asparagus on to boil.

1 tablespoon sea salt flakes	HOLLANDAISE
2 bunches fat asparagus	1½ cups (375 ml) verjuice
extra virgin olive oil, for brushing	1 bay leaf
freshly ground black pepper	6 black peppercorns
	250 g unsalted butter
	4 egg yolks

To make the hollandaise, combine the verjuice, bay leaf and peppercorns in a stainless steel saucepan, then bring to the boil and reduce over high heat to 2 tablespoons of liquid. Set aside.

Gently melt the butter in a small saucepan over high heat and cook for 5–6 minutes or until nut-brown, then remove from the heat. Pour the butter into a jug, leaving any residual brown solids behind in the saucepan. Set aside to cool for 10–12 minutes (if you have

Grilled asparagus with verjuice hollandaise

a digital thermometer, the temperature should register 69°C). Once it's cool, skim off any white scum floating on top, then carefully pour the clear liquid that remains into another small saucepan, leaving behind as much of the milky-white sediment as possible.

Bring a deep saucepan of water to the boil and add the salt. Break off the woody ends of the asparagus spears and discard them. Place a bowl of iced water by the stove, ready for refreshing the asparagus. Blanch the asparagus by plunging it momentarily into the boiling water, then quickly transfer the asparagus to the iced water, leave to cool, then drain.

Heat a chargrill plate over high heat, brush the asparagus with a little olive oil, season with pepper, then chargrill.

Place the egg yolks and cooled verjuice mixture in a small food processor and process to emulsify. With the motor running, add the nut-brown butter a little at a time until fully incorporated. Check the sauce for seasoning and add salt and pepper, if desired.

Place the asparagus on a plate and serve with a large dollop of the hollandaise.

CHEONG LIEW'S SALT WATER DUCK ACCOMPANIED BY ASPARAGUS

Serves 4–6, depending on size of ducks

This salt water duck is served at room temperature with warm asparagus and a Japanese-style mayonnaise – together they make a great meal. As the duck requires curing for three days, and then needs to steep in the stock overnight, you will need to start this recipe at least four days before you wish to serve it. Dried mandarin peel, dried liquorice root and rice vinegar can be found in Asian supermarkets.

⅓ cup coarse salt

1 tablespoon Sichuan pepper

2 ducks

sea salt flakes

2 bunches asparagus

1 teaspoon cumin seeds

1 teaspoon Sichuan pepper

5 g dried liquorice root

2 cm piece ginger, bruised

2 spring onions

WHITE MASTER STOCK

2 cups (500 ml) boiling water

100 g sugar

1 star anise

1 cinnamon stick

3 pieces dried mandarin *or* tangerine peel
   (each the size of a 50 cent coin)

JAPANESE-STYLE MAYONNAISE

125 g sugar

2 teaspoons Keen's dry mustard

50 ml rice vinegar

2 egg yolks

2 cups (500 ml) extra virgin
   olive oil, warmed

In a small frying pan, dry-roast the coarse salt with the Sichuan pepper for a few minutes, until you can smell the perfume of the pepper coming off the pan. While still warm, rub the salt and pepper mix into the ducks, using 1 tablespoon of the mix for each kilogram of duck. Leave to cure for at least 3 days in the refrigerator.

To make the stock, combine all ingredients in a saucepan. Bring to the boil, then simmer over low heat for 30 minutes. Strain the stock through a sieve into a large stockpot.

Submerge the cured ducks in water and leave for 1 hour. Blanch each duck momentarily in a large saucepan of boiling water and refresh it in a bowl of iced water. Put the ducks into the master stock and poach for 20 minutes over medium heat. Leave the ducks to cool in the stock, then refrigerate overnight.

To make the mayonnaise, combine the sugar with 125 ml water in a small saucepan and slowly bring to the boil, then simmer to reduce by about a fifth. In a bowl, make the powdered mustard into a paste with 1 tablespoon of this sugar syrup and slowly mix in the vinegar, then add the remaining sugar syrup. Stir in the egg yolks. Slowly pour the warm oil into the mixture and mix as you would a mayonnaise. Taste and add more vinegar if necessary.

Bring some salted water to the boil in a shallow flameproof roasting or sauté pan. Snap the ends off the asparagus, then lay them in the pan and simmer over medium heat for about 3 minutes if they are thin, and 6 minutes if they are thick.

Carve the duck from the bone and serve with the warm asparagus and mayonnaise.

BEETROOT

OVER THE YEARS AT THE PHEASANT FARM RESTAURANT I DEVELOPED
a keen sense of what my favourite customers liked. As they would sometimes drop
in without warning when they had guests staying, it was a matter of some pride
that I always managed to cater to their needs. Bob McLean (Big Bob), formerly of
St Hallett winery and then a restaurateur himself for some time at barr-Vinum in
Angaston, hates parsnip with a passion, and as I often teamed parsnips and game
I always had to make sure I had potatoes on hand so I could give him mashed spud instead.
And the pet hate of local artist Rod Schubert, whose work adorned the walls of the restau-
rant, was anything citrussy to end the meal, as the strong taste would all but ruin his
favourite tipple to match with a dessert, one of Peter Lehmann's stickies.

But it was Peter's wife Marg's love of beetroot that led me to use this root vegetable in
many different ways – she didn't mind how it was prepared, just as long as she could have
beetroot. This was no hardship for me as I adore beetroot too. It has a natural affinity with
game; in fact, the earthy sweetness of all root vegetables sits well with the richness of these
meats. Looking through our old menus, I notice that as well as offering beetroot as a side
vegetable, it was an integral part of many dishes that included guinea fowl, pheasant,
rabbit, hare, pigeon and kangaroo. It also featured strongly with offal, especially smoked
tongue (I tossed grated raw beetroot in butter over high heat and deglazed the pan with
a good red-wine vinegar).

Beetroot is available all year but is at its very best in its natural season, from winter to
late spring. Buying beetroot at its best means buying it with the leaves still attached.
Nothing gives you a better indication of freshness than the vitality of the leaves – and you
also get two vegetables for the price of one (in fact the leaves are a much better source of
vitamins than the root). They are edible, as are the leaves of other root vegetables such as
turnips, carrots and fennel. Beetroot is closely related to silverbeet, and the green or red
leaves of the mature plant can be cooked in exactly the same way – quickly tossed over

Steak sandwich with beetroot and rocket mayonnaise (see page 18)

high heat with butter and freshly ground black pepper is pretty good, but only if the leaves are sparkling fresh.

I try never to waste the leaves from tender young plants. I might chop the smallest and brightest and add them to a salad of warm waxy potatoes, or blanch them quickly and toss them through freshly cooked pasta with flat-leaf parsley, extra virgin olive oil, freshly ground black pepper and some grated mature goat's cheese.

Beetroot is one of those vegetables we take for granted, but a steak sandwich or a hamburger just wouldn't be the same without it. My favourite steak sandwich includes freshly

cooked beetroot, lashings of caramelised onion, some peppery beetroot or rocket leaves and a good dollop of rocket mayonnaise. Much as I prefer home-cooked fresh beets, I'll admit to keeping a few tins just in case.

Like so many vegetables, beetroot reveals another dimension when it is used straight from the garden. I have just been out and harvested a huge bunch of beetroot that were all planted at the same time. Those plants that were showing perhaps a third of their beets above the ground are large and the skin is dry and marked. Those that were totally buried are the size of a large apricot and their skin, which hadn't seen the light of day until I pulled out the plants, is flawless.

Smaller beetroot like these are sweeter and less likely to be woody. However, unless the grower is satisfying a niche market for 'baby' vegetables, beetroot of different sizes are often bundled together to achieve an average weight per bunch. This is not always convenient for the cook – not only do different sizes require different cooking times, but it is also more attractive to have beetroot of a similar size in one dish.

I'll make a raw salad from the small ones to savour their sweetness. All that's needed is a good vinaigrette of 3–4 parts extra virgin olive oil to 1 part red-wine vinegar (the ideal ratio will depend on the intensity of your vinegar), some salt and freshly ground black pepper, a little Dijon mustard, a splash of orange juice and some chopped garlic. As the staining ability of beetroot is legendary, this is one time when those disposable gloves you see people behind deli counters wearing come in handy. Peel the beetroot and grate it on a stainless steel grater. Toss the vinaigrette through the salad and add fresh herbs – chives or salad burnet are particularly good.

Care needs to be taken when cleaning beetroot in preparation for cooking. If you tear the skin, disturb the fragile root or cut the leaves off too close to the root, the beetroot will 'bleed' and masses of colour and flavour will be lost. Presuming you have lovely fresh tops on your beetroot, cut them a couple of centimetres above the root and use them as soon as possible. A gentle wash will rid the root and leaves of any residual dirt.

The most common method of cooking beetroot is to boil it in salted water, which can take anything from half an hour to an hour and a half, depending on size. A dash of vinegar added to the cooking water rids the beetroot of the peculiar soapy taste it can develop when boiled if it's not super-fresh. Don't be tempted to pierce the beetroot with a skewer to check for doneness as this too will make it bleed. Instead, take a beetroot from the water and let it cool slightly before squeezing it: if it gives a little, it is cooked. Once all the beetroot are just cool enough to handle, simply slip the skins off by rubbing them gently. I like to present small beetroot with about a centimetre of their tops in place, so I'm careful when doing this. (If you do stain your hands, it will come off with lemon juice, although whether every trace of pink vanishes immediately will depend on how many beetroot you've handled.)

I often bake rather than boil beetroot, as I find the flavour more intense. Pack the beetroot into an enamelled baking dish just large enough to hold them in a single layer and drizzle over extra virgin olive oil, then add a tablespoon of water and tuck in a sprig or two of thyme. Cover the dish with foil and cook the beetroot at 220°C for 40–60 minutes. These beetroot can be served in their skins or peeled as above. Beetroot can also be baked wrapped in foil and served with a dollop of sour cream and a sprinkling of chopped chives, just as you would a potato.

Garlicky aïoli or skordalia, a Mediterranean bread-based sauce, have to be among the most luscious accompaniments to beetroot. Try a salad of still-warm roasted beetroot, rocket and crisp pancetta served with grilled quail and a dish of aïoli. If going meatless, add melted goat's cheese to the rocket, along with some witlof, and finish off the salad with a wonderfully aromatic walnut oil vinaigrette and a few roasted walnuts. Or serve freshly cooked beetroot with skordalia made with roasted walnuts rather than the usual potato, and verjuice instead of water. Good crusty bread to go with it is mandatory.

Home-cooked beetroot need only a simple vinaigrette of good red-wine or balsamic vinegar, a little Dijon mustard, extra virgin olive oil and freshly ground black pepper to make a great salad. For a warm salad, try tossing diced baked beetroot with roasted garlic cloves, a freshly opened tin of anchovies, and a red-wine vinegar, orange juice and extra virgin olive oil vinaigrette.

Newer hybrid varieties such as golden or candy-striped beetroot look wonderful and provide an especially interesting effect when cooked and used in a salad. The variety called 'bull's blood' is an incredibly dark, purply black and the sweetest beetroot I've ever eaten, particularly when just picked. A word of caution, however. As much as I love raw beetroot – I often use the traditional purple beetroot grated raw in salads – I tried the same with a golden beetroot recently to disastrous effect. Colin and I tasted just a teaspoon of it and within minutes both our throats were burning so badly that we had to drink milk to try to ease the sensation. Even gargling with milk produced little result; it was a good 45 minutes before the burning subsided. My friend Stephanie says she hasn't found this problem, so perhaps this was an isolated instance.

Toss beetroot with nut-brown butter and freshly ground black pepper for the simplest vegetable dish. Another option is to mash slightly softened unsalted butter with lots of freshly chopped herbs – try chives and basil or thyme – and a little garlic, a squeeze of lemon juice and some freshly ground black pepper then toss it with hot, peeled beetroot. Or use the Barossa combination of cream and red-wine vinegar, which is often added to a warm potato salad. Bring 75 ml cream to the boil and add 1 tablespoon red-wine vinegar and let it amalgamate, then pour the sauce over hot, peeled beetroot (this amount of dressing will do for about 500 g beetroot). For a change, halve the amount of red-wine vinegar and add some mustard.

Beetroot is well known as the main ingredient in borscht (see opposite), a Russian soup that can be served hot or cold. Although I love beetroot, I find this soup rather too intense unless served with lots of sour cream or crème fraîche. On the other hand, beetroot makes a delicious sauce or purée, and one in particular remains firmly in my mind. Gay Bilson, Janni Kyritsis and the staff at Berowra Waters Inn cooked a wonderful meal entirely on portable burners on a disused wharf in 1986 during the first Sydney Symposium of Gastronomy. The highlight was the hare, rare and juicy, served with a beetroot purée. From my notes (I always take notes at great meals), I see that it was made with beetroot, onion, tomato concasse, cream and balsamic vinegar.

HORSERADISH-FLAVOURED PICKLED BEETROOT
Makes 500 ml

Beetroot pickles well, particularly when strong flavours such as fresh horseradish or mustard are used. A handy relish to have on hand as a last-minute accompaniment, this goes well with barbecued kangaroo or lamb loin chops (the latter with the fatty bits left on and allowed to char).

750 g beetroot	freshly ground black pepper
sea salt flakes	1 tablespoon sugar
400 ml red-wine vinegar	4 cloves
1 clove garlic, thinly sliced	6 coriander seeds
¼ cup freshly grated horseradish	

Cut the tops off the beetroot, leaving at least 2 cm. You'll need to clean the beetroot thoroughly as some of the cooking liquid will be reserved for later use. If the beetroot is very dirty, soak it in water rather than scrubbing the skin. Boil the cleaned beetroot in a saucepan of water over low–medium heat with 1 teaspoon salt and a little of the vinegar added (depending on size and age, beetroot can take as long as 1½ hours to cook). Remove the cooked beetroot from the cooking liquid and allow to cool a little before peeling. Strain the cooking liquid through a fine-meshed sieve and set it aside.

Coarsely grate the beetroot. Mix the garlic and the grated horseradish into the grated beetroot and season with salt and pepper. Tip the beetroot mixture into a hot, sterilised (see Glossary) glass or earthenware jar. Boil the remaining vinegar with an equal amount of the reserved cooking liquid, and the sugar and spices, in a non-aluminium saucepan for 5 minutes. Pour this hot solution over the beetroot, making sure it is just covered (if more liquid is needed, boil equal amounts of water and vinegar and add to the jar to top up – these must be added in a 1:1 ratio to prevent the growth of harmful bacteria). Seal the jar and allow it to mature in the pantry for 2 weeks. Refrigerate after opening.

RAW BEETROOT SALAD WITH ORANGE RIND   *Serves 4*

This salad is an excellent accompaniment for barbecued kangaroo fillets.

1 bunch small red beetroot, trimmed,
    washed and peeled
rind of 1 small orange, cut into fine strips
¼ cup flat-leaf parsley leaves
1 tablespoon lemon juice

⅓ cup (80 ml) fruity green
    extra virgin olive oil
sea salt flakes and freshly ground
    black pepper

Grate the beetroot as finely as possible to yield 2 cups; the finer the beetroot, the more luscious the salad. Toss the grated beetroot, orange rind and parsley together. Whisk the lemon juice and olive oil together and dress the salad, then season with salt and pepper.

BORSCHT   *Serves 4*

I return to my desire for the simple by giving you my not-very-authentic version of borscht, a hearty soup that can be served hot or cold (I prefer it cold). When made from freshly dug beets, it can be exceptional. This soup is best not reheated as it tends to lose its colour.

butter, for cooking
extra virgin olive oil, for cooking
2 large onions, roughly chopped
6 beetroot (about 150 g each),
    peeled and cut into chunks
pale inner heart of 1 bunch celery, chopped

sea salt flakes and freshly ground
    black pepper
1.5 litres Golden Chicken Stock
    (see page 159) *or* vegetable stock
1 tablespoon red-wine vinegar
chopped dill, to serve
sour cream *or* crème fraîche, to serve

Heat some butter in a large saucepan with a little olive oil over medium heat until nut-brown, then sweat the onions until soft. Add the beetroot and celery heart and sauté for a few minutes, then season and cover with chicken or vegetable stock. Reduce heat to low and simmer for about 2 hours.

Purée in a food processor or blender and add the red-wine vinegar. Allow to cool and then chill soup in the refrigerator. Serve cold topped with fresh dill and a dollop of sour cream or crème fraîche.

BEETROOT SAUCE FOR KANGAROO, PIGEON OR HARE *Serves 4*

500 g beetroot

6 golden shallots, thinly sliced

1 sprig thyme

extra virgin olive oil, for cooking

1 teaspoon Dijon mustard

2 tablespoons cream

2 tablespoons reduced veal stock

sea salt flakes and freshly ground
   black pepper

balsamic vinegar, to taste

Preheat the oven to 220°C. Cut the tops off the beetroot, leaving at least 2 cm. Wrap the beetroot in foil, then bake for 40–60 minutes. Remove the beetroot from the foil and allow to cool a little before peeling. Purée the beetroot in a food processor.

Sweat the shallots with the thyme in a little olive oil in a saucepan over low heat for 10–15 minutes until softened. Add the beetroot purée, mustard, cream and stock and check for seasoning, then add balsamic vinegar to taste. Serve immediately.

CUMQUATS

THE CUMQUAT, OR KUMQUAT, IS A VERY SPECIAL FRUIT TO THOSE who appreciate its many uses in cooking, as well as its ornamental beauty. There is nothing like the simple beauty of a cumquat tree in a large terracotta pot in a north-facing courtyard. Cumquats were grown commercially in South Australia many years ago, but found not to be profitable, and as far as I can tell don't appear to be grown on a commercial scale anywhere in Australia now other than at The Kumquatery in Renmark, owned by Andrew and Patria Kohler (previously known as Tolley's Nurseries). As an eating fruit, they are really an acquired taste, and unfortunately it's not financially viable to grow them just for jam-making. It comes back to the age-old dilemma of what should be developed first – a market or an orchard?

Commercial purposes aside, Ian Tolley, the well-known, now-retired Renmark nurseryman of Tolley's Nurseries, says the important factors in growing cumquat trees, either in the ground or in pots, are reasonable drainage and consistent watering. In his many years of working with citrus fruit, the problem he was most often asked about concerned splitting fruit. The fruit splits when trees are allowed to dry out, then are over-watered, then allowed to dry out again. The cumquat is not strictly a citrus but is grafted to a dwarf citrus rootstock to limit its size to half that of an orange tree in an effort to improve the quality of the fruit. As a small tree it is often grown in pots, making the problem of drying out particularly relevant. All citrus trees do better with good drainage, although there are special rootstocks available for marginal drainage situations. The main thing is not to allow them to dry out.

Fertilising is important and two reasonable applications per year are recommended. It is better to use slow-release blood-and-bone, or Complete D, rather than inorganic fertilisers. It isn't necessary to put it through a dripper system, which is expensive and difficult. Simply spread it around the tree, scratch it in, and water with a sprinkling hose.

Ian describes the cumquat as a 'precocious bearer' because it yields some fruit in the second or third year, and a reasonable crop in six to eight years. In Renmark, the season runs from the end of August until the end of November.

Cumquats in sugar syrup (see page 26)

One of the reasons that the cumquat has not succeeded commercially in the past was that it was deemed suitable only for jam or glacé fruit, and the larger glacé manufacturers weren't interested, probably because of the cumquat's small size, as well as the number of seeds. Work to reduce the number of seeds in cumquats is slowly progressing. This is happening mainly through growers identifying trees that produce fruit with fewer seeds and letting nurseries grow stock from them. Talking with Ian about one of my favourite topics – cooks working directly with growers – I became quite excited about the possibilities, until he told me that the development of seed-free cumquats would mean reduced crop and fruit sizes. Sometimes it simply makes more sense to quit while you're ahead!

Even though commercial glacé manufacturers had spurned the cumquat, I persuaded Ian's wife, Noëlle Tolley, that there was a market for her homemade glacéd cumquats. I had the pleasure of taste-testing all her trials and her product was nothing short of sensational. One kilogram of glacéd cumquats went a long way, and I featured the fruit on the restaurant's dessert menus as often as I could. They added a great dimension to a silky buttermilk panna cotta or crème brûlée, and their glaze starred in an Almond and Cumquat Tart (see page 30) – what a winner. I also find that this glaze makes a wonderful basting liquid for slow-cooking ducks.

The two varieties of cumquat Noëlle and I worked with were the marumi, which has a sweet rind, and the nagami. The marumi is delicious eaten fresh, picked straight from the tree, and I prefer it glacéd for desserts, but the nagami, when prepared with less sugar, is an ideal accompaniment for game. Noëlle once sent me some cumquat slices that had been dried, using no sugar at all, in a dehydrator rather than in the sun. I found the flavour wonderful for stocks with poultry or venison. It is truly exciting to see products of such quality.

And the Tolleys, even though retired, planted more cumquat trees and were selling their dried and candied cumquats under the brand name Kumquaterie. They also produce a cumquat glaze and a mince 'krumble', as Noëlle calls it, from imperfect cumquat halves. The name Kumquatery remains with the new owners.

More than any other fruit, cumquats are offered to me by non-cooking gardeners at a loss as to what to do with their crop, feeling that they have neither the time nor the skill to make jam. I take advantage of such windfalls and am compelled to try as many options as possible to show that there's more to cumquats than just jam.

Having said that, cumquat marmalade is a joy – possibly even better than my much-loved Seville marmalade, and it's a cinch to make. Quarter the fruit and leave it to soak overnight just covered with water. The next day, measure the fruit with a cup into a heavy-based saucepan, then cover the fruit with the soaking water and cook until it is tender but still intact. Add the same number of cups of sugar as you did fruit, then boil rapidly until the mixture is set. To test this, place a spoonful onto a saucer and put in the fridge for a few minutes. Then test the marmalade by pushing it with your finger – if it wrinkles it is set. To make a smoother, less chunky marmalade, cook the cumquats whole and then cut them in half and remove their pips. Purée the cooked pulp in a blender, then simmer it with sugar until it reaches setting point.

Cumquat butter is wonderful to use when cooking poultry or rabbit. Chop cumquats finely, removing the pips, then work the fruit into softened unsalted butter with chopped herbs. The choice of herbs will depend on what you are cooking and what you have to hand: rosemary or thyme are particularly good. Stuff the mixture under the skin of a chicken or duck breast (a Muscovy duck, which doesn't have a great deal of fat, works well) – the butter bastes the meat as it cooks, keeping it moist and leaving the skin golden and crisp.

Whole or peeled cumquats (if you have time on your hands and don't like the bitter skin as much as I do) cooked slowly in a sugar syrup (see Glossary) can be added to a moist, pudding-style cake. Serve this with a spoonful or two of clotted cream alongside. Allow a flourless chocolate cake to cool and then cut it in half carefully (it will be flat and dense). Halve the syrupy cumquats, remove pips, then dot the cut surface of the cake with them. Put the top back on the cake, then coat it with chocolate ganache. Cumquat marries with chocolate even better than orange does.

Or try pricking ripe cumquats once or twice with a needle, placing them in a sterilised glass jar (see Glossary), adding a little sugar if you have a sweet tooth, and then covering them with brandy. Leave them for a year – if you are strong enough to resist.

I was interested to learn that in the Philippines there are few lemons available and people actually prefer to use sliced green cumquats in drinks. The greener and more bitter the fruit, the more they enjoy it. They also squeeze ripe cumquats for juice in the same way as we squeeze oranges, and use the juice of green cumquats on noodles, where we might use lemon. They also combine soy sauce with cumquat juice (in roughly equal quantities, to get that balance of salt and sour) to serve alongside fried fish or chicken. And they use cumquats for medicinal purposes – the lukewarm juice of grilled cumquats is a remedy for an itchy throat after persistent coughing.

CHICKEN AND TARRAGON SAUSAGES WITH CUMQUATS *Serves 4*

I can't emphasise enough the importance of using good-quality sausages. I am lucky to be able to use my daughter Saskia's chicken sausages, which are made entirely from chicken meat and skin and the fat of the chicken when bred to maturity.

30 g unsalted butter

12 thin or 8 thick chicken and
    tarragon sausages

8 cumquats, sliced into 3 or 4 widthways
    and pips removed

½ cup (125 ml) Golden Chicken Stock (see
    page 149), or more depending on pan size

1 tablespoon chopped French tarragon
    or chervil sprigs

sea salt flakes and freshly ground
    black pepper

In a heavy-based frying pan large enough to hold all the sausages in one layer, melt the butter, then gently seal the sausages and cumquats over medium heat until the sausages are just browned, without pricking the skins. Add stock, then bring to a simmer, cover and cook gently for 5–7 minutes or until sausages are cooked through. Remove the sausages and set aside in a warm place, then quickly reduce the pan juices over high heat to a sauce consistency. Add the herbs and season to taste, then serve immediately.

SASKIA'S WEDDING CAKE   *Serves 50*

This is such a special recipe from a very special ex-staff member, Natalie Paull, one of the 'extended family' of talented youngsters who came through the Pheasant Farm Restaurant kitchens, and whose lives I have been fortunate enough to stay connected with as they go on to do great things of their own. Nat had an unshakeable path in life, and while still at school in Sydney, wrote me a beautifully penned letter to ask if she could come over and do work experience with me. It was one of those requests I couldn't refuse, especially from one so young. There was no doubt that Nat had talent right from the start, and her time working with me was such a vital period in the life of the restaurant.

I've already written about the highs of the last four months of the restaurant, after we had announced that we were closing down, and what an incredibly exciting time it was coping with the huge numbers of people who wanted to come one last time. Our elder daughter Saskia had planned her wedding for a week after we closed, so that we would have time to recover from the closing 'wake', which was one continuous party on 28 November 1993, finishing at five o'clock the next morning, which also was our younger daughter Elli's eighteenth birthday. This gave us time to cook for the wedding free of restaurant commitments, and the gang of three, Nat, Alex Herbert and Steve Flamsteed, stayed around so they could help and be part of the festivities.

Nat cooked this truly wonderful cake for Saskia's wedding. How I wish I'd recorded all the food of the event as it was a great feast, only some of which I remember. Then, going through boxes of memorabilia recently I found Nat's handwritten notes for this recipe – yet another gift from her. She started her own dessert business called Little Bertha in Richmond, and now has Beatrix in North Melbourne, where she makes the most delectable treats, including the stunning La Marjolaine, a dessert we used to make in the restaurant days. Even though I profess to have no sweet tooth, I did used to find myself in the coolroom suspiciously often – just checking!

According to Nat's notes, this recipe makes one large 28 cm and one medium 22 cm round cake, each of which stands about 5 cm high. It serves about 50 people as a celebratory treat. I recommend that all the ingredients be at room temperature for the best possible results. The method and amounts for the fruit layer can be adapted for any kind of dried fruit; you could use raisins and dried figs instead of the cumquats and infuse the butter cream with vanilla instead of orange-blossom water, as this would be amazing too. The cake would be just as wonderful to eat with a cream-cheese icing or even a ganache, which would go well with the cumquats.

This cake keeps well for up to three days. »

580 g butter, softened

580 g castor sugar

12 × 55 g eggs, at room temperature

1 teaspoon vanilla extract

460 g plain flour

200 g self-raising flour

pinch salt

CUMQUATS

375 g dried cumquats

185 ml boiling water

200 ml dessert wine

BUTTER CREAM

9–10 egg yolks (180 g)

finely grated rind of 2 oranges

225 g castor sugar

1 cup (250 ml) light corn syrup

675 g butter, softened

1 tablespoon orange-blossom water

2 tablespoons Cointreau *or* other
orange-flavoured liqueur

Soak the dried cumquats in a bowl of just-boiled water overnight, covered with plastic film. The next day, add the dessert wine and cook uncovered in the microwave on high for two 6-minute bursts, stirring between each. Leave to cool completely.

Preheat the oven to 150°C. Lightly grease a 28 cm and a 22 cm round cake tin with melted butter, then line the bases and sides with baking paper and set aside.

Cream the butter and sugar in an electric mixer on medium speed until pale and fluffy. Add the eggs slowly, about 2 at a time, beating between each addition, until all the eggs are incorporated, then add the vanilla extract. The mixture may start to curdle a little at the end of this process, which is why it is important to start with room-temperature ingredients.

Transfer the batter to a large bowl. Combine the flours and salt in another bowl. Sift the dry ingredients over the top of the batter, then gently fold the flour in thoroughly. Weigh out 1 kg of the batter and transfer it to the prepared 28 cm cake tin, then weigh and transfer 500 g of the batter into the smaller cake tin, reserving the rest. Spread the batter out, making it a little higher at the sides of the tins. Scatter two-thirds of the cumquat mixture over the batter in the large tin and the remaining cumquats over the batter in the smaller tin. Spread the remaining cake batter over the cumquats in both tins.

Bake the cakes for 75 minutes, then cool them in the tins, before turning out onto wire racks to cool completely.

Meanwhile, for the butter cream, whisk the egg yolks and orange rind together in an electric mixer. Place the sugar and corn syrup in a saucepan and bring to the boil over high heat. As soon as the syrup boils, transfer it to a heatproof jug; if you have a sugar thermometer, the syrup should be at 116°C or the soft boil stage. Working in 3 batches, immediately pour one-third of the syrup into the egg yolk mixture, then beat on high speed for 30 seconds. Turn the mixer off before adding the next batch of syrup as the beaters will spray the mix around the sides of the bowl and it will not incorporate properly. Mix in the last 2 batches, beating in between, then beat the mixture on high speed until cool. Add the butter in 6 batches and allow each batch to be taken into the mixture before adding the next. Stir in the orange-blossom water and Cointreau. This butter cream can be made in

advance and freezes beautifully. When ready to use, defrost it fully in the fridge, then soften to spreading consistency in a microwave; take care not to overheat or the mixture will separate.

Spread a thin layer of butter cream over each cake and refrigerate for 1 hour (this is called a crumb coat and hides any uneven surfaces or dark patches on the cake). Then spread enough icing over the crumb coat to fully cover the cakes. The cakes are sturdy enough to tier, if you wish, without the aid of a high-tech support structure.

Store and serve at room temperature as the butter cream is best when not refrigerated.

ALMOND AND CUMQUAT TART   *Serves 8*

The Kumquatery sells cumquat glaze through specialty outlets in South Australia and Victoria, but it is not widely distributed and it's difficult to make unless you have lots of cumquat trees, so substitute with a strong honey such as leatherwood or mallee, or even imported chestnut honey.

6 cups (960 g) almonds	GLAZE
1 × quantity Sour-cream Pastry	175 g bitter chocolate
(see page 151)	¼ cup (60 ml) rich double cream
1 teaspoon ground cinnamon	1½ tablespoons cumquat glaze *or* honey
1 tablespoon finely grated cumquat rind	1 tablespoon brandy
½ cup (125 ml) brandy	60 g unsalted butter
1½ cups (375 ml) cumquat glaze *or* honey	
125 g unsalted butter, softened	
mascarpone mixed with a little grated	
cumquat rind and juice, to serve	

Preheat the oven to 200°C. Roast the almonds on a baking tray in the oven to release their flavour, leave them to cool, then grind in a food processor. Reset the oven temperature to 175°C. Make the pastry as instructed, then roll out to line a 22 cm tart tin. Refrigerate until required.

Mix the ground almonds with the cinnamon and cumquat rind. Stir in the brandy, cumquat glaze or honey and butter. Pat this mixture into the tart shell and dot with butter. Bake for about 30 minutes or until the crust is golden. Leave to cool at room temperature.

To make the glaze, heat the chocolate, cream, cumquat glaze or honey and 1 tablespoon water in the top of a double boiler until the chocolate has melted. (If you don't have a double boiler, use a heatproof bowl that fits snugly over a pan of boiling water.) Remove from heat and stir in the brandy and butter. Smooth the glaze over the tart with a spatula. Do not refrigerate.

Serve with mascarpone with a little finely grated cumquat rind and a dash of juice stirred through it – be careful not to make the mascarpone too runny.

BUTTERMILK PANNA COTTA WITH CUMQUAT SAUCE

Serves 6

4 × 2 g gelatine leaves (see Glossary)

400 ml cream

150 g castor sugar

1 cup (250 ml) buttermilk

CUMQUAT SAUCE

600 g cumquats, halved and seeded

400 g castor sugar

1 cinnamon stick

Soak the gelatine leaves in cold water to soften. Combine the cream and sugar in a saucepan over medium heat and bring almost to the boil. Squeeze the excess moisture out of the gelatine and whisk into the cream mixture, then add the buttermilk. Turn the heat to low, otherwise the buttermilk may split. Divide among six 125 ml moulds and place in the refrigerator to set overnight.

To make the cumquat sauce, combine all ingredients in a saucepan with enough water to cover the fruit (about 500 ml). Bring to the boil, then reduce heat to low and simmer for 1 hour, adding more water if necessary. Set aside to cool. Remove cinnamon stick before using.

Serve the panna cotta topped with a spoonful of cumquat sauce.

EGGS

ALTHOUGH EGGS ARE A SIMPLE FOOD, THEY ARE FULL OF SOUL.
When we ran the restaurant we had a goose that made a nest in the same spot
every year on a little strip of earth in front of the restaurant (in full view of
table three). She would lay her egg at around lunchtime every day, which is much later
than normal. I was convinced that she did it because she liked the attention of the customers, who were obviously enchanted by her. She was never successful with her 'sitting', as
she liked to put on a show by going for a swim in the middle of lunch, leaving the nest for
a lot longer than a good mum should. Once she had a nest full, she sat there for the whole
of spring in the vain hope that the eggs would hatch – usually the smell of rotten eggs
would remind us that it was time to take over from nature and chase her away.

Now that we have gone full circle – starting with opening the Farmshop way back in
1979, then running the restaurant for nearly fifteen years, now back running the Farmshop
again on the old restaurant site – instead of a goose, it is one of the wild peacocks who
takes up that position most days. Not because *he* is laying an egg, but because it is obviously
a very desirable spot for a bird that craves attention.

It became obvious to me what a difference a good egg makes when Stephanie Alexander
and I held our cooking school in Tuscany. We were encouraging a group of students to
make pasta by hand. It was about 35°C and the humidity was high. The villa kitchen was
too hot for pasta-making, so we moved upstairs to make the dough in an ancient marble
sink, not just for its coolness but to contain the mess created by a dozen enthusiastic cooks.
The yolks of our eggs were the colour of gold, and the silky pasta we had kneaded long and
hard was now a shiny ball, in spite of the heat. Everyone was marvelling at how clever they
were – until I reminded them that the ingredients they had been working with probably
had something to do with their success, too.

The cry that 'eggs don't taste like they used to when we had our own chooks' has been
familiar to me ever since I moved to the Barossa some twenty years ago. In fact, chook

eggs didn't rate at the Pheasant Farm Restaurant. Instead, it was duck, goose, pheasant, guinea fowl or quail eggs. The yolks of these exotic eggs were so rich it was as if they had been injected with a creamy mayonnaise.

Until my time in Italy, I hadn't thought much about this, as we always had my friend Hilda's eggs when our daughters were young and used our farm eggs for the restaurant, so we seldom resorted to commercial chook eggs. But after Italy I was determined to have our own chooks on our home property. This is when I discovered that it's not enough to give them a proprietary feed. What you feed them, and the greens they have access to, will have a huge impact on flavour and colour. If you have your own chooks, you will be struck by the difference between these and mass-produced eggs. Now, thankfully, free-range eggs with their deep-gold yolks and good flavour, which result from a combination of the grain they are fed and their ability to pick grass and insects, are available to all. However, they will still only be as good as the food the chook eats. If any hen's diet is supplemented by fish meal, that's how the eggs will taste. We need eggs to taste like eggs, not fish. I react so badly to commercially produced fried eggs when breakfasting away from home that I often wonder whether they are off, until I recall this.

Eggs are certainly one of the more versatile foods we have. They are marvellous on their own (think of a soft-boiled egg perched in an egg cup with toast soldiers or brown bread to dunk – still the food I crave when overtired, even for dinner), and they can be cooked in a variety of ways: soft-boiled, hard-boiled, poached or fried. Eggs combine well with other ingredients, either using the richness of the egg yolk with olive oil or butter to make Mayonnaise (see page 148), my Aïoli (see page 49), Hollandaise (see page 12) or béarnaise; or whole eggs, which are integral to custards, quiches, soufflés, omelettes, frittatas, and pasta and cake dough.

Every restaurant faces the question of leftover egg whites – how many meringues can you make? We used to put egg whites into dated and numbered containers in the fridge, hoping for an excuse to use them. I sometimes wonder if the Brownies or Scouts, instead of having a 'bottle round', could collect egg whites and make confectionery to sell.

Eggs are easier to beat in a copper bowl with a whisk than having to take out the electric mixer and then wash it all up afterwards. You are less likely to overbeat the eggs this way, and the copper bowl gives the whites a creamier, yellowish foam. The same eggs beaten in a mixer or stainless steel bowl will be snowy white and drier.

A meringue can be both over- and under-beaten. Soft meringues should be baked at 180–190°C for 15 minutes. This crisps the surface and leaves the interior moist and chewy.

Hard meringues are baked at 100°C for up to 2 hours, or left overnight after being placed in a hot oven, which is then turned off just as you put them in. If they leak syrup or collapse, it is because they are undercooked. If they have beads of syrup on the surface, they have either been cooked at too high a temperature or the sugar didn't dissolve properly.

It is not just egg whites that are whipped. Whipped yolks are added to various breads and cakes to contribute to the yolky flavour or to help reinforce a foam. Sabayon is a warm, frothy, rich mixture of yolks, sugar and Marsala (or you can use verjuice).

Tips for peeling hard-boiled eggs would have saved me hours of anguish in the first few years of our business, when in the evening I would sit and peel bucket after bucket of quail eggs. My daughters Saskia and Elli were only four and two years old when we began farming quails, a year before we started the Farmshop. I used to sit with a bucket between my legs and the girls either side of me. We had a book propped on a chair and I would read to them, my hands in the bucket as they turned the pages. They used to love to eat the yolks if I tore the egg white, but they don't often eat eggs now – I wonder why! Looking back, I don't know how I managed this for so many evenings over so many years. After four years we contracted the job out and life started to improve.

The most important tip for hard-boiled eggs is that they should not be too fresh for boiling, because the fresher they are, the harder they are to peel. Preferably they should be one week old. For pickling, boil quail eggs for 6 minutes – you need to use a wooden spoon to move the eggs around in the water so that at their 'setting point' the yolks will be in the centre of the egg. The skins of quail eggs are much tougher than those of chook eggs. They are difficult to peel and if the yolk is too close to one end of the egg, the skin will be torn and the egg useless. The moment the eggs come out of the boiling water they should be quickly thrown into iced water to cool. To peel, pick up the egg and crush the pointy end against the table so that the whole shell crazes in your hand. The skin should slip off in one piece.

Soaking the eggs overnight in vinegar dissolves the outer membrane of the egg shell and makes it very easy to peel. This is only useful if you are going to pickle the eggs rather than have them fresh, as the vinegar flavour is so strong. It is also expensive and plays havoc with your hands.

Freshly boiled quail eggs (boiled for only 2–3 minutes), peeled and cut in half lengthways and topped with caviar, make wonderful hors d'oeuvres.

I have often wondered why quail or chook eggs sometimes have a greenish-grey discolouration on the surface of the yolk. It happens mostly with less-than-fresh eggs (I noticed it with the quail eggs, of course, because I was using them not so fresh for ease of peeling). I then discovered, while reading Harold McGee's book *On Food and Cooking,* that the colour is caused by a harmless compound of iron and sulphur – ferrous sulfide – which is formed only when the egg is heated. Minimising the amount of hydrogen sulfide that reaches the yolk will reduce the discolouration: cook the eggs only as long as necessary to set the yolk and then plunge the eggs immediately ionto cold water and peel them promptly. Overcooked hard-boiled eggs will be grey around the yolk.

SCRAMBLED EGGS AND CAVIAR
Serves 3–4 for breakfast

Cooking scrambled eggs may be an art form, but serving them with smoked salmon and salmon roe, or with caviar as I've done here, elevates them to the luxury class. Then there are sea urchins: since rediscovering my taste for sea urchin roe after eating a sea urchin custard in Paris a few years ago now (which scored an 'ultimate experience' rating), I like to simplify the combination of eggs and sea urchin by adding the roe to scrambled eggs. When I do this, I press the roe of four sea urchins through a fine strainer, then whisk it into the egg mixture and season to taste, or simply drape the 'tongues' of roe over the just-cooked scrambled egg. After cooking, I divide the eggs among the cleaned sea urchin shells, then top with a little salmon roe and serve with rye toast and unsalted butter. This recipe is also good served with thick slices of smoked salmon.

The classic combination of eggs and caviar or sea urchin roe can also be served in little tartlets as a canapé or entrée, but be sure to use good buttery flaky pastry.

6 free-range eggs
¼ cup (60 ml) rich double cream
sea salt flakes and freshly ground
   black pepper

30 g unsalted butter
as generous an amount of caviar as you can
   afford *or* the finely grated rind of
   1 orange

Whisk the eggs and cream together, and season with salt and pepper. In a heavy-based frying pan, melt the butter and as it heats pour in the egg mixture and lower the temperature. Scrambled eggs must be only just cooked, so keep on a low temperature and avoid stirring too much until they begin to set, then use a plastic scraper to gently pull the cooked edges into the centre. Remove the pan from the heat when the eggs are about three-quarters done, then stir very gently so that just the residual heat of the pan finishes the cooking. They must be moist and creamy. Serve immediately, piled high with the caviar or scattered with orange rind.

CRÈME CARAMEL

In the very early days of the Pheasant Farm Restaurant, the menu was *table d'hôte* – in other words, our guests had no choice at all. Whilst this may not have suited everyone, no one was ever disappointed with dessert. Although it changed according to the fruits in season, our 'never-fail' standard was a large crème caramel, served as individual slices with extra caramel on top. We used our own eggs, and always cooked the caramel to a bitter counterpoint to offset the custard's richness. We found making it the day before was important for it to properly set; we would then turn it out on to a large plate and slice it into wedges as if it were a cake.

For years we made individual serves in our export kitchen. Getting the caramel right every time is a tricky procedure, as even though we make all our products in much greater numbers now, I use exactly the same principles as I did in the restaurant kitchen long ago.

CARAMEL
½ cup (110 g) sugar
125 ml water

CUSTARD
4 large eggs
145 g castor sugar
1½ cups (375 ml) milk
190 ml cream
1 vanilla bean, halved lengthways

To make the caramel, use a small heavy-based saucepan to dissolve the sugar in the water over low–medium heat. Leave it until the mixture turns a very deep amber colour (just one step before burning) and pour into four 120 ml-capacity individual soufflé moulds or ramekins, turning them so the caramel coats the sides.

To make the custard, lightly beat together the eggs and sugar and cover with a cartouche (see Glossary) until needed.

Preheat the oven to 180°C. Heat the milk and cream in a saucepan with the scraped vanilla bean seeds and the bean itself, then bring to scalding point. Cool slightly. Gradually pour this over the egg mixture, stirring carefully. Strain the combined mixture through a fine sieve into another bowl to remove any large strands of egg. Carefully pour the custard into the dishes, over the caramel.

Place the dishes in a roasting pan two-thirds filled with hot water and bake for 25 minutes or until set. Allow the crème caramels to cool in the water bath, then remove from the pan, cover with plastic film and refrigerate.

Serve the following day, turned out onto plates. If you want to make extra caramel to pour over the crème caramels to serve, simply make another batch of the caramel, using the quantities and instructions from the start of the recipe.

PICKLED QUAIL EGGS

36 quail eggs, at least 1 week old	1 level teaspoon black peppercorns
1½ cups (375 ml) white-wine vinegar	1 level teaspoon allspice berries
50 g sugar	1 fresh bay leaf

Place the quail eggs in a saucepan and cover with cold water. Stir them gently with a wooden spoon until they come to the boil. Boil the eggs for 5–6 minutes and tip them straight into iced water to cool. This not only inhibits further cooking, but makes the job of peeling much easier. Tap the pointy end of the egg on the bench and gently crush the shell with your fingers; that way, once you have taken off the first bit of shell, the rest falls away.

Place the peeled eggs in a large sterilised jar (see Glossary). Boil the other ingredients together in a saucepan for about 5 minutes, until the sugar has dissolved and all the ingredients are combined, and then pour them over the peeled eggs. The vinegar has such a low pH level that the eggs will keep for months at room temperature.

These eggs are delicious tossed in a salad, or cut in half and served with some salmon roe sprinkled on top.

GOOSE EGG CUSTARD TO SERVE WITH MULBERRIES   *Serves 4*

If you have a mulberry tree, preserve some of the surplus fruit to try with this dish, as the combination of flavours is wonderful.

2 goose eggs	1 vanilla bean, halved lengthways
2 tablespoons castor sugar	butter, for greasing
1 cup (250 ml) milk	preserved mulberries (optional), to serve
1 cup (250 ml) cream	freshly grated nutmeg, to taste

Preheat the oven to 120°C. Lightly beat together the eggs and sugar and cover with a cartouche (see Glossary).

Heat the milk and cream in a saucepan with the scraped vanilla bean seeds and the bean itself, then bring to scalding point. Cool slightly. Gradually pour this over the egg mixture, stirring carefully. Strain the combined mixture through a fine sieve into a baking dish lightly greased with butter.

Put the dish in a roasting pan and pour in hot water to reach halfway up the sides of the dish. Bake for 1–1½ hours. Remove from the oven and allow to cool in the pan. Serve with preserved mulberries, if using, and garnish with freshly grated nutmeg.

FLAT-LEAF PARSLEY

AFTER YEARS OF ABUSE, PARSLEY ALMOST BECAME A DIRTY word in my kitchen parlance. It was the token garnish of a sprig of curly parsley with the tired slice of orange found on almost every plate in the 1970s that made me reject this herb in any form for many years. It wasn't until we bought our farmhouse in 1987, and discovered a garden well established with a parsley very like the flat-leaf variety you can buy now, that I started to look on parsley more kindly. My opinion is so changed that when my daughter Saskia, who is a caterer, was planning a herb garden, I urged her to plant parsley, parsley and parsley!

The flavour of flat-leaf parsley is sweeter and nuttier than the curly variety and it's the only one I consider growing or using. In fact, I would say it's the herb I use most often. However, I know this is a very personal stance, as curly parsley has a very distinctive flavour that many love.

A few culinary tips for parsley. When you pick or buy a bunch of parsley, put it in water as you would flowers. Parsley quickly goes limp otherwise and its flavour will be inferior. When instructed to chop parsley, normally you just use the leaves and reserve the stalks for stock, although if they are very young I often use them chopped really finely. Wash the parsley well and dry it in a salad spinner or tea towel before chopping, and only chop it just before you need it. *Never* keep leftover chopped parsley for use the next day – it will taste like lawn clippings! And I'd never chop parsley leaves super-fine. If you don't feel confident with a knife, try just plucking the individual leaves, particularly if you're adding the parsley to pasta.

The traditional bouquet garni used in stocks and stews is a bundle of fresh parsley, thyme and a bay leaf; the proportions change according to the desired flavour of the end dish. A bouquet garni can also include basil, celery, chervil, tarragon, salad burnet, rosemary or savoury. The herbs, tied together with string, are lowered into the simmering pan and removed before serving.

If you are making a sauce such as a hot vinaigrette to serve with fish or chicken, throw in some parsley at the last moment. The same goes for parsley added to a hearty winter soup or rustic stew. And don't under-rate the simple practice of sprinkling chopped parsley over pot-roasted meat or a bowl of soup topped with just a drizzle of your favourite extra virgin olive oil.

Parsley fried in nut-brown butter is a great accompaniment to offal. It can also be deep-fried: immerse the parsley in bubbling clarified butter for just a few minutes – the flavour is wonderful.

If you have parsley in the garden, you'll never be caught short. Make a vinaigrette to serve with hot or cold barbecued chicken or seafood by mixing equal quantities of chopped parsley and extra virgin olive oil with enough red-wine vinegar to provide balance, then add salt and lots of freshly ground black pepper. Anchovies or capers can be added as well. Steep grilled chicken breasts or steamed broccoli fresh from the garden in the vinaigrette before serving. Braised leeks and this vinaigrette make a good pair, too.

Gremolata – chopped parsley, crushed garlic and lemon rind – sprinkled over dishes such as osso buco or lamb shanks adds a wonderful zing, and is also good with boiled meats. Try a French classic by making a *persillade*, a mixture of chopped parsley, golden shallots and breadcrumbs, and pressing it over a roasting shoulder of lamb in the last 10 minutes of cooking. *Jambon persillade* is a traditional French dish I have always admired; the version I make is simply cubes of ham captured in a glistening jelly of verjuice set with gelatine leaves, with loads of fresh parsley – it is a wonderful warm weather dish.

To continue the French influence, parsley and garlic butter is, of course, served with snails. Try mixing 75 g softened low-salt butter, 2 tablespoons chopped parsley, 2 crushed garlic cloves, a little lemon juice, salt and freshly ground black pepper. As butter picks up refrigerator odours and quickly becomes rancid, freeze the parsley butter (without the garlic) in small quantities rather than refrigerating it. (Chopped raw garlic becomes unpleasant once frozen and will alter the flavour of the compound butter – add it to the butter after defrosting.)

A really green butter can be made by mixing finely chopped parsley, sorrel and the green parts of spring onions with butter, a dash of lemon juice and a grind of black pepper. Let a slice of this butter melt over veal scaloppine, brains, chicken, fish or potatoes baked in their jackets.

I love tossing fresh vegetables with parsley and extra virgin olive oil, especially small zucchini that have been cooked whole. I let the zucchini cool a little, then slice them lengthways and dress them with small freshly plucked parsley leaves, a drizzle of extra virgin olive oil and a grind of black pepper. Freshly dug baby waxy potatoes boiled and tossed with butter, a squeeze of lemon juice, salt, freshly ground black pepper and lots of just-chopped parsley is another great favourite.

You can make parsley essence by putting a bunch through your electric juicer: add this to thick, homemade mayonnaise for a refreshing accompaniment to cold seafood.

Parsley has a natural affinity with tomatoes and eggs. Dress slices of ripe tomato and just-hard-boiled free-range eggs with the parsley vinaigrette mentioned opposite. Toss vine-ripened sliced tomato with equal quantities of chopped parsley and basil. Or make tabbouleh by mixing lots of chopped parsley and mint with diced tomato, burghul, lemon juice and diced onion.

When I get home late and find nothing much in the cupboard for dinner, I sauté onion in extra virgin olive oil in a frying pan until it is translucent and then toss in wedges of ripe tomato for a few minutes before seasoning the lot well. I slip eggs into the centre of the pan to cook and then serve this wonderfully satisfying concoction with lots of chopped parsley and salt and freshly ground black pepper.

The only dishes I can remember hating in my childhood were white sauce and parsley with tripe or corned silverside, and parsley added to scrambled eggs. I've never quite recovered from the white sauce/parsley combination, but I now love perfect scrambled eggs with chopped flat-leaf parsley folded in at the last moment in the same way I do an omelette with parsley, chives and tarragon. (I also now adore tripe, especially cooked in the Italian way with loads of onions, tomatoes and parsley.)

PARSLEY, PRESERVED LEMON AND CAPERBERRY SALAD *Serves 4*

12 caperberries

1 cup flat-leaf parsley leaves

1 tablespoon thinly sliced preserved
  lemon rind

⅓ cup (80 ml) extra virgin olive oil,
  plus extra for shallow-frying

2 thick slices wood-fired bread, torn into
  bite-sized pieces

1 tablespoon red-wine vinegar

Slice 6 of the caperberries in half and put into a glass salad bowl, then add the parsley leaves and preserved lemon. Heat enough olive oil for shallow-frying in a frying pan over high heat, then add the bread and fry until golden. Remove with a slotted spoon, then add to the bowl, along with the olive oil, vinegar and remaining whole caperberries. Toss together so that the dressing soaks into the croutons, then serve.

WALNUT AND PARSLEY PESTO

Serves 4

If your garden is overflowing with parsley, try this variation of pesto, using parsley and walnuts ground with garlic and extra virgin olive oil, to serve with pasta and shaved Parmigiano Reggiano. This pesto is also delicious with smoked tongue.

2 cups (200 g) shelled walnuts	100 ml extra virgin olive oil
2 cloves garlic	2 teaspoons sea salt flakes
1 cup firmly packed flat-leaf parsley leaves	freshly ground black pepper

Preheat the oven to 220°C. Dry-roast the walnuts on a baking tray for 6–8 minutes, then rub off the skins with a tea towel and sieve away any remaining bitter skin. Allow to cool, then grind all the ingredients using a mortar and pestle or by pulsing in a food processor. The pesto will keep for a few days, covered with a film of oil, in a jar in the refrigerator. I invariably have difficulty preventing my pesto from oxidising after a few days, finding the recommendation to cover it with a film of oil never quite sufficient (although a splash of lemon juice will help if you are planning to store it). For this reason, when basil is abundant, I often resort to making a paste with the basil, pine nuts and oil and then freezing it in tiny plastic pots with a good seal. The pots can be defrosted in hot water and then mixed with the grated cheese and garlic (garlic shouldn't be frozen as its composition will change) and perhaps a little more oil and seasoning.

SALSA VERDE

Serves 4

Salsa verde, an Italian green sauce, is often served with boiled meat (it is the traditional accompaniment to *bollito misto)*, poached chicken breasts, fish or offal, and is especially good with tongue or brains.

1 boiled potato, peeled and chopped	extra virgin olive oil
1 cup firmly packed flat-leaf parsley leaves	1 tablespoon red-wine vinegar
3 anchovy fillets	sea salt flakes and freshly ground
1 clove garlic	black pepper
2 tiny cornichons (see Glossary)	

Combine the potato, parsley, anchovies, garlic and cornichons in a food processor. With the motor running, add enough olive oil, a little at a time, to make a thick sauce, then blend in the vinegar, salt and pepper. This sauce is best served on the day it is made.

GARLIC

WHEN YOU THINK OF THE IMPORTANCE OF GARLIC IN FOOD, IT IS no wonder it is celebrated. It is hard to think of a cuisine that doesn't embrace garlic. A garlic festival has been held in Tours in France on St Anne's day, 28 July, each year since 1838. More recently there has also been a garlic festival held each August in Gilroy, California. In her *Chez Panisse Café Cookbook*, Alice Waters talks at length about a garlic dinner she prepared for this festival. It is amazing to think of a whole menu using garlic. There were vegetables with garlic, Chinese garlic cakes, tortellini with garlic, fish with dried chillies and garlic, quail stuffed with whole garlic baked in grape leaves, and a Moroccan eggplant salad with garlic. Even the dessert was wine-spiced garlic sherbets. One might think that such a dessert was a novelty, devised to justify the inclusion of garlic, but Alice Waters' notes on the menu said that, 'The most memorable aspect of this meal for me was the garlic sherbets, which were made with red fruits macerated with red wine and garlic cloves, and with white fruits macerated with white wine and garlic cloves, to create a very fruity beginning flavour to the sherbet with a lovely garlic aftertaste.'

The whole issue of finding good garlic used to be really difficult in Australia. Now so many people appreciate the difference between imported garlic bleached white to kill bacteria and mould, and the fresh garlic from our own soils.

Indeed the organic movement has 'sprouted' interest in fresh, locally grown garlic. Often pink-striped, it appears in the marketplace around November and December. The flavour of this garlic is superb and makes a huge difference to a dish. So look for Australian garlic rather than the uniformly white imported garlic – the improvement in flavour is phenomenal, and Australian growers need to be encouraged.

Commercial producers who use chemicals to combat weeds plant garlic in February, while organic farmers plant in April or May. As a result, our garlic season is extended a little. Green garlic makes its way onto the market in early spring – this is an attempt on

the part of the farmers to make production more economically viable. These shoots look similar to leeks, as the bulb is yet to form and separate into garlic cloves, while the flavour has the familiar pungency of dried garlic. Green garlic is handy to use before the local, better-keeping dried garlic becomes available from late spring – the shoots are deliciously sweet when roasted whole and can also be added to salads.

Garlic is really easy to grow, and once pulled from the garden it can be hung to dry in your shed; it will then be available for months and months, if kept dry and cool.

In the Barossa, we have a fantastic Saturday-morning farmers' market. Years ago, two lads, the Marschall boys (as they are referred to, who began growing garlic when only in years ten and twelve at school), sold their crop of 1200 garlic plants in the first two

weeks of December, and they went on to double their crop the following year. The boys had been lucky enough to have Michael Voumard, a great chef and organic gardener of note, as a mentor. That garden is more like a wonderland, and its bounty is used in his cooking at Rockford Wines for the dining room of the Stonewall Club.

To prepare garlic, take the clove – pulled away from the bulb – and press down on it on a chopping board with the flat side of a large-bladed knife. This will pop the skin off, which you can then remove. Add a sprinkle of salt, continue applying pressure with the knife, and the garlic will become 'creamed' and ready for use, without any trace of bitterness. If you do not want to add salt, use a sharp knife to cut the clove into fine pieces. (Raw garlic is very powerful and the finer it is chopped or sliced, the stronger it will be.) Using a garlic press to crush garlic will make it bitter. Be careful when sautéing garlic as it burns easily and will then become bitter too.

What would bruschetta be without a cut clove of garlic rubbed over warm, toasted bread before the tomato, basil and a drizzle of extra virgin olive oil are added? The same goes for a salad, where rubbing the inside of the bowl with garlic before tossing the lettuce in leaves a subtle note. And raw garlic mixed with lemon rind and flat-leaf parsley is delicious with boiled meats.

I love roasting the whole garlic bulb, whether fresh or dried, and using it in many different ways. I don't know why slowly roasted heads of garlic have gone out of fashion. When Alice Waters wrote of them in her *Chez Panisse Menu Cookbook* in 1982, many kitchens across the land offered roasted garlic with goat's cheese, a crouton and olive oil – a classic combination. Roasted garlic, easily squeezed from its papery shell onto a crouton, is wonderfully sweet and nutty. Or the roasted head of garlic can be served whole, or cut in half horizontally.

When garlic is cooked it becomes rich, sweet and buttery and marries well with foods as diverse as lamb, kid, beef, quail, chicken, goat's cheese and eggplant. Either rub the whole bulb with some extra virgin olive oil and roast it in a 180°C oven with a little thyme, or try cooking it slowly in the smallest container possible, either in the oven or on top of the stove, totally immersed in olive oil or stock with sprigs of thyme, bay or rosemary. Remember, in both cases, to prick the bulb beforehand to prevent it exploding.

Green-striped garlic heads just pulled from the ground and roasted whole are incredibly sweet. Although fresh jumbo garlic can be very bitter, growers are beginning to select their largest corms for their planting stock rather than selling them to eat, which seems to be making a difference.

Slow-cooking suits garlic perfectly. If pot-roasting, add unpeeled cloves with the meat or poultry. Once the dish is cooked, squeeze the garlic from its skin into the juices – if there are enough cloves, they can become a purée to flavour and thicken the sauce.

While not all Italians use garlic and Italian food is not just about pasta, the partnership seems natural. Spaghetti with garlic, oil and chilli is comfort food for many. In winter, try combining chopped garlic with toasted walnuts, cream and Parmigiano Reggiano in a sauce to toss through fusilli. I cook masses of peeled garlic cloves slowly in olive oil for about 20 minutes until they're golden, then toss these through wide pasta ribbons with caramelised fennel, preserved lemon and a generous amount of flat-leaf parsley and freshly ground black pepper. Shavings of Parmigiano Reggiano and a drizzle of extra virgin olive oil finish off this delicious combination of flavours.

Patricia Wells, in her book *At Home in Provence*, also combines garlic with preserved lemon, but this time in a dish with rabbit. Whole heads of garlic with the top third cut away are cooked cut-side down, and the preserved lemon melts into the cooking juices. Patricia also writes about garlic soup, where a head of garlic combines with leeks, onions, golden shallots, bouquet garni, potatoes and herbs. Elsewhere she describes cooking fresh white beans with garlic, fresh bay leaves and thyme, and suggests simmering a head of garlic in cream and adding the resulting purée to mashed potato.

The French are keen on using garlic in sauces. If a strong flavour appeals to you but you're trying to stay away from eggs, make an Authentic Aïoli (see page 49). Or make garlic butter by mixing roasted garlic together with unsalted butter cut into small portions, and keep it in the freezer (this prevents rancidity) to add richness to a sauce at the last minute.

I once wrote on garlic in a weekly column in *The Advertiser*, when I first started writing about food, and I received letters from readers asking what to do about garlic preserved in olive oil turning blue. I contacted the CSIRO and they told me the following about the dangers of holding garlic or similar products in oil.

The main cause of the problem is the level of acidity. The outer leaves of garlic, and to some extent the bulbs themselves, may contain anthocyanin pigments, which are colourless at the normal pH of garlic but turn blue or even pink under acid conditions. Most garlic cloves do not contain sufficient quantities of this pigment for the discolouration to pose a problem. Test each batch of garlic by adding vinegar to a small sample of garlic and warm it. If it discolours, seek out another supply of garlic.

At the same time the CSIRO made me aware of incidents of botulism in the United States involving garlic in oil products. Oil has no antimicrobial preservative action – its only function in preserving is to prevent oxidisation which can lead to discolouration of some foods. By excluding oxygen from the surface of vegetables, one is establishing anaerobic conditions, which actually favour the growth of some types of bacteria, one of which is *Clostridium botulinum*, the organism which causes botulism.

It is therefore essential that sufficient acid, usually in the form of vinegar, be added to the vegetable before oil is poured on, so that these bacteria cannot grow. This means that the pH level must be reduced to below 4.6. Mass-produced vinegars usually contain about 5 per cent acetic acid. Any mixture should therefore have a vegetable to vinegar ratio by weight not greater than 3 to 1, which would give 1 per cent acetic acid, ensuring that the final pH is below 4.6.

ROUILLE
Makes 400 g

A pungent and particularly more-ish way of using garlic is to make this paste to serve with a fish soup, stew, braised oxtail, lamb shanks or with a crudité of fresh vegetables. For those who like spicy heat, it can be adjusted by including a chilli with the red capsicum. *Rouille* is French for 'rust' – and this should be the colour of your sauce.

1 large, very red capsicum	4 cloves garlic
200 ml extra virgin olive oil, plus extra for roasting	50 ml red-wine vinegar
	a few saffron threads (optional)
2 slices bread, crusts removed	3 free-range egg yolks
milk, for soaking	sea salt flakes and freshly ground
½ teaspoon cayenne pepper	black pepper

Preheat the oven to 200°C. Cut the top off the capsicum and remove the seeds. Rub with some olive oil and roast in the oven until it collapses and seems to be burnt – usually about 20 minutes. Take the capsicum from the oven and let it rest for a few minutes before putting it in a plastic bag to sweat. When it is cool enough to handle, peel, removing all traces of blackened skin.

Soak the bread in a little milk for 10 minutes, then squeeze it thoroughly.

Place the capsicum, cayenne pepper, garlic, bread, vinegar, saffron threads, if using, and egg yolks in the bowl of a food processor and purée well. Season, then with the motor running, slowly pour in the olive oil in a stream as you would for mayonnaise, processing until emulsified.

AUTHENTIC AÏOLI

Makes 1 cup

Aïoli is a garlic mayonnaise – a garlic lover's dream. It is a very important dish in Mediterranean cooking and a great accompaniment to something like octopus which has been marinated in extra virgin olive oil and lemon juice and then thrown on the barbecue.

A young man with a Catalan background once spent a few weeks in my kitchen, and from him I learnt that original aïoli in its purest form contains no eggs, is white and shiny, and very strongly flavoured with garlic. It is also said to be impossible to make a true aïoli in a food processor as the oil and garlic become too homogenised. So, for a truly authentic aïoli, take out your mortar and pestle.

6 cloves garlic, green shoots discarded,   **½ teaspoon salt**
    finely chopped   **1 cup (250 ml) extra virgin olive oil**

The ingredients should be at room temperature. Mash the garlic using a mortar and pestle, mixing in the salt until it is a thick paste. Add the olive oil very slowly, a few drops at a time, and always stir in the one direction with the pestle. Continue adding the oil slowly until an emulsion forms. Serve immediately.

MAGGIE'S AÏOLI

Makes 1 cup

I am more at home with the way I have always made aïoli – with eggs. I have calmed down about the amount of garlic I use these days and would now only use 2 cloves to every 250 ml extra virgin olive oil, but those who really want to have that hit of raw garlic I believe can use up to 6 cloves. At times I roast the garlic before adding it to the mayonnaise, in which case it could be called roasted garlic aïoli. For this, I would use 6 or more cloves of garlic, as its flavour when roasted is sweet and nutty.

2 cloves garlic, or to taste   **2 free-range egg yolks**
½ teaspoon salt   **1 cup (250 ml) extra virgin olive oil**

Mash the garlic using a mortar and pestle, mixing in the salt until it forms a thick paste. Add the egg yolks, then proceed with adding the oil, remembering to proceed very slowly until at least one-third of the oil has been used. Continue adding the oil slowly until an emulsion forms. Serve immediately.

GOAT'S CHEESE

SPRING AND SUMMER MEAN LOTS OF GOAT'S MILK FOR MAKING cheese. As long as there is enough rain to provide green feed, goat's milk is at its most plentiful from October to March. During the winter months some dairies taper off production whilst others use frozen milk to maintain supplies.

Will Studd, a man who knows more about cheese than anyone else in Australia, tells me that goat's milk has smaller fat globules than cow's milk and so is more easily digested. He also says goat's cheese can be eaten late at night without the need for lots of red wine to break it down, as with other cheese – a theory many would relate to.

The person who first made us all take notice of Australian goat's cheese is the wonderful Gabrielle Kervella from Western Australia, who began the Kervella Fromage Fermier label. A now-retired farmer and cheese-maker, she was a passionate advocate for goat's cheese – and we have a lot to thank her for, since pioneering is never easy. Gabrielle took her passion one step further and became an organic producer.

Many others Australia-wide have followed the trail-blazing Gabrielle in making high-quality goat's cheese. John Wignall of Tasmania's tiny but important Bothwell Dairy makes goat's cheese that is sold within the island state, as do one or two other small producers, such as Nick Haddow of Bruny Island Cheese, who is making some incredibly exciting cheeses and, small as their operation is, they are already exporting to great acclaim. South Australia is very proud of Woodside Cheese Wrights, whose Edith cheese was first established by the original makers, wine-maker Paula Jenkin and chef Simon Burr, bringing together technical ability and an innate understanding of flavours. The company, which produces a range of cheeses made from goat's and cow's milk, has gone from strength to strength and is now run by Kris Lloyd. Their Edith cheese is sold in an ashed round, as both Paula and Simon learnt to make it that way in France. In October, when the milk supply is plentiful again, Woodside makes Capricorn, a creamy goat's milk camembert and many more. Another South Australian contender making really good goat's

cheese is Udder Delights – as small companies need to, they are always innovating. And Pino Marmorale at La Vera Mozzarella, a third-generation cheese-maker from Naples, makes a three-year-old matured goat's cheese that I marvel at.

Julie Cameron of Meredith Dairy in Victoria is another cheese-maker worthy of mention. As part of her range she makes fromage blanc and fromage frais, neither of which is salted, and so can be used in sweet as well as savoury dishes. She takes the top layer of the milk, where the cream settles, to make the blanc, a cheese that can be served individually and tends to be marinated (as I do with grappa on page 56) or used as a dessert dish. The fromage frais is the body of the milk drained of whey; it is used mainly on pizzas or in vegetable terrines. Also from Victoria, Laurie Jensen of Tarago River Cheese Co. makes Childers, a particularly wonderful goat's cheese camembert, as well as Strzelecki Blue.

Then there's Richard Thomas, who was such a significant player in the industry since its beginnings, and whose influence on the development of cheese-making in this country has been immense. His past credits include stints at King Island, Kangaroo Island, Milawa, Meredith and Gippsland, and over the years he has developed some of Australia's finest cheese varieties. He started the Yarra Valley Dairy in 1996, and has worked with so many people, sharing his passion and knowledge.

The Yarra Valley is now a wine and cheese mecca, with All Saints Estate and Giant Steps Winery also selling handmade cheese in addition to their wines. And Holy Goat Organic Cheese, east of Castlemaine, is making seriously good goat's cheese, from fromage frais to more mature varieties. Ann-Marie and Carla of Holy Goat Cheese have become the benchmark for all that is great in this industry – with the pinnacle being their La Luna cheese.

It is wonderful to be able to write that I cannot keep up with all the good producers who are appearing. As each region attracts passionate producers who are driven to maximise their potential, produce of all kinds just gets better and better.

The range of quality goat's cheeses today is quite extraordinary and it has indeed become a special part of our food life. It is such a versatile cheese and you have to do so little to present it as part of a meal – just remember to take the cheese out of the refrigerator well in advance so that it can come to room temperature first, otherwise its flavour won't be fully developed.

One of the great advantages of goat's cheese is that it makes a great entrée or luncheon dish, whether simply melted on croutons as part of a salad, cubed and tossed with roasted pumpkin, walnuts and rocket, or stuffed in the centre of roasted and peeled red capsicums. As a main course, toss it through pasta with zucchini flowers and anchovies, adding crunchy roasted almonds for texture; or layer pasta sheets with goat's cheese, eggplant and roasted tomatoes. The list of possibilities is endless, as goat's cheese marries so well with Mediterranean flavours: slowly roasted garlic, olives, anchovies, capers, eggplants, ripe tomatoes, peppery salad greens, walnuts and walnut oil.

Serve fromage blanc (without added salt) alongside poached fruit, as I so often enjoyed while travelling through the French countryside and eating at small country restaurants.

No sugar was added, yet the cheese was sweet but piquant. Fromage blanc also works well wrapped in vine leaves and grilled – the cheese oozes out and the leaves caramelise. All these parcels need is a drizzle of extra virgin olive oil and a sprinkling of salt and freshly ground black pepper – let them cool a little, then devour them with crusty bread.

A tip if you are cooking goat's cheese – do not leave it in the oven or under the griller once it has melted, as it will become grainy and separate with prolonged heating.

To prove my point about the versatility of goat's cheese, let's start with goat's curd, a younger, softer version of the mature cheese. Surround the curd with your best young salad leaves; make a hole in the centre of the soft curd and fill with your best walnut oil. Serve with crusty bread – walnut bread would be best of all – sea salt and freshly ground black pepper and you've got a meal.

Curd is great for ravioli fillings. Drain it if it seems too moist, then mix chopped semi-dried tomatoes, basil leaves, sea salt and freshly ground black pepper and make little parcels of fresh pasta. You could add a sauce of very ripe chopped tomatoes, a little seasoning and a fruity extra virgin olive oil, or simply drizzle with just enough extra virgin olive oil to moisten the ravioli once cooked. Or mix goat's cheese with finely chopped cooked eggplant or mushrooms, or poached asparagus or artichokes, and use to fill fresh ravioli.

For something more substantial, place thin slices of pancetta on a baking tray and crisp quickly in the oven as you heat goat's cheese on croutons. Serve the croutons with the pancetta and strips of baked or shallow-fried eggplant on top. The same applies to roasted red capsicums, cut into strips. Drape them over the croutons, with anchovies or olives, and add lots of chopped flat-leaf parsley and extra virgin olive oil.

Stuff zucchini flowers with tiny knobs of goat's cheese, kneaded with roasted pine nuts and drizzled with olive oil. Coat them in a tempura-style batter, shallow-fry quickly and serve immediately.

A good dried pasta cooked and served with roasted garlic cloves, cubes of goat's cheese to melt over the hot pasta, flat-leaf parsley and extra virgin olive oil makes a truly great meal without fuss. Add and subtract as you like with any of the season's flavours. Don't forget, the goat's cheese left at the back of the fridge that has become truly matured and hard as a rock can simply be grated over hot pasta in the same way as Parmigiano Reggiano.

Goat's cheese and pastry are another time-honoured combination. Try a savoury tart – start with a rectangle of baked Sour-cream Pastry (see page 151), spread generously with a soft goat's cheese and topped with caramelised onion, then returned to a 180°C oven for about 10 minutes, before serving with a final flourish of extra virgin olive oil and lots of peppery salad greens.

In very late spring you may be able to pick the first of the figs in hotter climes: layer sliced ripe figs with goat's cheese and basil, seasoning as you go with extra virgin olive oil and freshly ground black pepper, then serve with crusty bread. Or make a simple 'sand-wich', which Chris Manfield, originally from Adelaide but whose fame has now spread much further afield, made famous during her days at the Paramount Restaurant in Sydney: her simple layering of deep-fried eggplant rounds, strips of roasted capsicum, freshly made pesto and fresh goat's cheese is just a great combination.

Goat's cheese featured at 'the wake' held the day the Pheasant Farm Restaurant closed, 28 November 1993, a wonderful event stage-managed by our friend Rod Schubert. The

invitation to attend was an amazing version of Lewis Carroll's classic 'The Walrus and the Carpenter' read by Kate Jordan-Moore, an old team member. The sun was beginning to hit the hills on the far side of the dam and we wanted everyone to experience the light of the early evening sky reflected in the water as we had drinks (a scene familiar to the Wednesday table and other Barossa lunch groups). At exactly 7.45 p.m. Bob McLean and Rod Schubert lit the candles in the large cande-labra in a corner of the restaurant, then Bob, he of the loud voice, called everyone in. At 7.50 p.m. the light flooded into the room, as did all our guests.

Rod had positioned four life-sized figures around the room: plaster-of-Paris bodies with glass mannequin heads, as seen in shop windows many years ago. One was sentinel at the end of a huge table that groaned with food; two were at the front windows; and another, dressed in a Pheasant Farm Restaurant T-shirt and long white apron, was by the table with the cutlery and crockery at the back of the room. The perfect 'silent' waiter! Almost in the centre of the food, right next to the suckling pig surrounded by pickled figs, was an up-ended elegant plaster leg. All these figures were spot-lit as dark descended, lending an ethereal feel to the room. Huge arrangements of flowers abounded – Aileen, their creator, must have stripped her garden bare.

My favourite tipple at the time, Yalumba's 'D' sparkling wine, flowed and the staff, wearing newly made T-shirts, black as usual with the gold pheasant on the front but with 'Ain't going to work on Maggie's Farm no more' in gold on the back, passed around baskets of delights. Labna made from goat's milk yoghurt was rolled into bite-sized balls and arranged on vine leaves with preserved wild olives, asparagus spears, prosciutto and olive bread croutons. Another basket, again lined with vine leaves, boasted olive bread and dishes of caperberries, sliced pickled quinces and more wild olives, plus a huge bowl of goat's curd doused with extra virgin olive oil. A basket of yabbies shared the limelight with boletus mushrooms I had preserved in the autumn, accompanied by caramelised garlic cloves, a dish of extra virgin olive oil and wedges of lemon.

On the table were masses of just-out-of-the-oven loaves of bread that Nat and Alex, two of my 'extended family' of staff, had made using dried muscatels. Bowls of duck egg pasta with olive paste and herbs or smoked kangaroo and pine nuts sat alongside. Eggplants, baked quail and couscous, leek tarts, sorrel tarts, octopus, more yabbies, oysters, tongue with salsa verde, pheasant pies and lots of salads of bitter greens all fought for space.

The festivities had several stages: the drinks beside the dam, the feast itself, and then the party after most of the guests had left, well after midnight. The after-party celebration was twofold, as the date we closed the restaurant had been chosen very particularly. It was the day before Elli's eighteenth birthday and the week before Saskia's wedding, which gave us time to prepare for another feast. Closing the restaurant, which had been my obsession in life but had taken so much of my time during most of their lives, was my gift to the girls. So at midnight Elli's party and the staff party began. We'd had music to begin the night, but the tempo changed now as Steve Grant, another ex-staffer, played the acoustic guitar and sang his heart out as we danced. At 5 a.m. we called it a night, exhausted but happy.

You don't need a feast to have an excuse to make labna. It's perfect as a nibble, with salads or as an accompaniment to lamb, kid or poultry, particularly if you also add strips of preserved lemon. Labna is really just cheese made from goat's, sheep's or cow's milk yoghurt (choose a naturally made one as some of the commercial brands are too thin). It's important to buy a thick yoghurt, and then mix 1 kg yoghurt with 1 teaspoon salt, and pour this into a muslin or Chux-lined sieve or colander and let it drain over a bowl in the refrigerator overnight, or if you want it firm enough to shape into balls, make it two days before using it. (In the winter you can hang the muslin 'bag' over the tap in the kitchen sink.) Form the drained yoghurt into bite-sized balls, then roll these in chopped herbs and drizzle with extra virgin olive oil before serving, Alternatively, add chopped rosemary or oregano, preserved lemon and roasted garlic cloves to the labna and cover with olive oil until required.

MARINATED GOAT'S CHEESE

Serves 4–6

When I first read of the idea of marinating goat's cheese in grappa, in Michele Scicolone's book *The Antipasto Table*, I couldn't wait to try it. I found it absolute dynamite with garlic and parsley. As a drink, grappa, which can be bought in specialist Italian groceries, is something I think you have to be born to, but here its fruity aggressiveness is balanced by the creaminess and sweetness of the unsalted cheese. If the goat's cheese you are using is more acidic, try using something smoother than grappa, perhaps Cognac.

1 large clove garlic, finely sliced

2 tablespoons grappa

⅓ cup (80 ml) extra virgin olive oil

⅓ cup roughly chopped flat-leaf parsley

freshly ground black pepper

2 × 180 g tubs Kervella *or* Meredith
Dairy Fromage Blanc

Combine the garlic, grappa, olive oil, parsley and a few coarse grinds of pepper. Pour a little of this marinade into a glass or ceramic dish, then gently add the cheeses and pour the remaining marinade over them. Cover the dish with plastic film and place in the refrigerator for 24 hours to marinate, turning the cheeses once or twice.

Serve the cheeses, removed from the marinade, at room temperature with rocket dressed with extra virgin olive oil and a good balsamic or aged red-wine vinegar. Slabs of bread, brushed with extra virgin olive oil and toasted in the oven, are a must.

CROUTONS WITH GABRIELLE'S GOAT'S CHEESE, SALSA AGRESTO AND ROCKET

Serves 6

To make this a little more substantial, you could also add roasted garlic cloves, walnuts and prosciutto to the peppery rocket salad.

1 baguette, sliced diagonally

extra virgin olive oil, for cooking

6 handfuls rocket leaves, trimmed,
    washed and dried

red-wine vinegar, for drizzling

250 g Kervella Fresh Goat's Curd

1 × quantity Salsa Agresto (see page 151)

Preheat the oven to 200°C. Brush one side of the baguette slices with olive oil and toast in the oven until golden. Dress the rocket with a little of the extra virgin olive oil and vinegar.

Pile the croutons with goat's cheese and top each one with a dollop of salsa agresto, then serve with the rocket salad.

PASTA WITH BROCCOLINI, PANCETTA, GOAT'S CURD
AND TOASTED BREADCRUMBS

Serves 4

I like to serve this when the pasta is warm enough to melt the goat's cheese just a little.

1 cup (70 g) firmly packed breadcrumbs, made from stale wood-fired bread

extra virgin olive oil, for drizzling

2 tablespoons chopped flat-leaf parsley

finely chopped rind of 1 lemon

24 thin slices pancetta

1 bunch broccolini

500 g penne

180 g goat's cheese, cut into 1 cm pieces

sea salt flakes and freshly ground black pepper

2 tablespoons lemon juice

Preheat the oven to 200°C. Place breadcrumbs on a baking tray and drizzle over 2 tablespoons olive oil, then roast until golden brown. Mix with the parsley and lemon rind. Bake the pancetta on baking trays for about 5 minutes or until crisp, and set aside.

Cook broccolini in a shallow pan of boiling salted water for 3–5 minutes, then drain and drizzle with olive oil.

Cook pasta following the directions on the packet and then drain. In a large bowl, toss the hot pasta with the warm breadcrumbs, pancetta and broccolini and the room temperature goat's cheese. Season, then add lemon juice and olive oil to taste.

HONEY

ONE OF THE SPECIAL TREATS OF LIVING ON THE FARM AND having space around us was being able to wander down to the creek on a warm evening, with a glass of sparkling wine in hand, to visit the beehives. We baby-sat the hives of our friend Nigel Hopkins for a couple of years. After he reclaimed them, we missed them so much that I bought my husband Colin an antiquated beehive to restore (however, it is still sitting in the shed awaiting repair as daily life and the more urgent matters of the farm and business took over). Its restoration is still on our 'must do' list, as it was such a special thing to lie in front of a hive and be part of its hypnotic hum of activity. (Nigel tells me the hum is the sound of the bees, having had a full day of nectar-gathering, fanning their wings to evaporate any moisture.) The sweetness of the air combined with the humid perfume of the honey is truly one of the most magical smells in the world. It is such a soothing experience – I can truly recommend it to anyone who is at all stressed.

Honey is becoming a scarce commodity, as there are fewer areas in which apiarists are allowed to keep their hives. Honey is normally 'fined' to remove any of the sediment that occurs when it is collected – mind you, I love it as it comes, with bees' knees and all. Bottling the honey without warming it excessively is a very slow process. Warming the honey makes it easier to bottle, but some of the flavour is lost. It is almost impossible to bottle honey without warming it at all, but passionate beekeepers try to keep it to an absolute minimum. There is a huge difference between honey prepared this carefully and ordinary commercial honey.

Pure honey direct from the beekeeper is becoming rare. Being a natural product with nothing added, honey will crystallise at cooler temperatures. The crystallisation can be reversed by heating the jar on the lowest setting in a microwave or by placing it in a roasting pan half-filled with water in the oven for a few minutes. You can then pop the jar of honey in the fridge for a short time to thicken it up again if you like.

In the past, local Barossa apiarists Mark and Gloria Rosenzweig of Moculta provided the honey for the Farmshop from their static apiary, the only one of its kind in Australia. Their honey is very beautiful, although as customers will not buy honey if it's starting to crystallise, we had to avoid it in the winter. It has a fantastic consistency: well-rounded on the palate, with floral overtones from the Salvation Jane plants that the bees pollinate. The under-note is from the Mallee honey myrtle tree, and is almost butterscotch in flavour. It has a gentle sweetness yet is not oversweet, which suits my palate.

The individual hives are kept in a long, very narrow, L-shaped corrugated-iron shed; the shed is roofed and also closed to the weather on the outer edge. Boxes stand on planks suspended from beams by metal rods, each passing through a pot of sump oil to keep ants at bay. These boxes are quite different from the hives that open from the top that you see in stacks in the countryside. Instead, each box has a glass window in front that allows the apiarist to check the activity inside; a door on the side gives access to the frames that carry the honeycomb, and the front has a landing platform for the bees.

My first visit to them years ago was on a very hot, windy afternoon, and the bees were angry. Mark is allergic to bees, so no one was taking any chances when it came to gathering the honey. We all donned beekeepers' outfits to keep rogue bees at bay and Mark was armed with a smoker. Bees sense fear and can turn on those emitting it. For some reason I have never been fearful of bees – not lying in front of our hives and not there in the shed.

Nothing modern interrupted the activity in the shed, yet the honey flowed perfectly: a turkey feather brushed away the groggy bees and a century-old, hand-forged knife with a curved blade was used to slice off the wax capping the cells. Gloria lifted a frame, and the gold of the honey dazzled us as she slipped it into the old separator (bought second-hand at auction in the early 1900s by Mark's grandfather for 2 shillings and sixpence!). It was during this first visit that I thought how much I'd like to have access to the Rosenzweigs' honey: their traditions are so intact and the hives, honey room and associated equipment make it a living museum well worth preserving.

Kangaroo Island is unique for many reasons, one of them being that it is the oldest bee sanctuary in the world. Ligurian bees were introduced there in 1884, the following year a sanctuary was declared and since then no other bees have been brought to the island. The Kangaroo Island Ligurian bee is disease-free, exceptionally quiet, easy to handle and produces good honey. The native bees on the island do not produce honey and do not interbreed with the Ligurian, which is checked continually to ensure that it is true to type.

There is still today a strong trade in Kangaroo Island queen bees. The bees can be tricked into making extra queens but it requires a great deal of effort on the part of the beekeeper. The queen bees are then sent to apiarists around the world in wooden boxes the size of a match box. Each queen bee is fed on the journey by eight worker bees (these are known as escorts!) from supplies of honey and icing sugar. (This is the one instance when the worker bee is on 'light duties', as she – all the males are drones – usually spends half of her six-week-long life cleaning out the frames and the other half gathering nectar.)

I believe Australian honey to be among the purest and tastiest in the world, with only honey from New Zealand and Canada coming close. Our native trees lend their own particular scents and characters to the honey, as do introduced strawberry clovers and citrus blossom; spring is the peak time for blossom. Buy different honeys to assess which ones you like best. Try pale, mild blue-gum or sugar-gum honey, or gutsy leatherwood honey and full-flavoured red-gum, mallee or bottlebrush honey. The leatherwood honeys of Tasmania are particularly distinctive – they are not for the faint-hearted but they're an absolute favourite of mine as, even though it may sound strange, some honeys are too sweet for me. And one of my other favourites is orange-blossom honey, but the aromatics fade so quickly I have to make the most of it when it's at its peak in December. Lavender also produces a sweetly scented honey.

The difference between honey direct from the apiaries and much of the honey found in supermarkets (although there are definite exceptions) is pronounced – I'd equate this super-market honey with cask wine. It's the bottom of the range and made by big producers: blended from different varieties, the honey is heat-treated and filtered very finely to achieve the maximum degree of 'user-friendliness'. Most producers, big and small, heat honey to help them bottle it, but the good ones keep the heat low enough so that the flavour is less affected. Very fine filtering removes some of the pollens and, along with them, some of the flavour. Consumers tend not to cope with bees' knees, wings and pieces of wax in their honey, but this thick, luscious honey straight from the hive is my favourite.

There is honey that falls somewhere between generic honey, which is always runny and has plenty of sweetness but no finesse or character, and the honey that I prefer, which can threaten to bend a spoon but has masses of flavour. Some larger producers pay premium prices for high-quality honey from small beekeepers and keep the varieties separate, meeting the rigid standards of ISO 9002 accreditation yet keeping the honey as close as possible to the optimum. Look for those companies that make named honeys – those that declare the plant source. And look out for signs advertising honey for sale when travelling in the country – you may be lucky enough to find unfiltered, and may even be able to buy honeycomb.

Creamed honey is simply runny honey that has been beaten with a little naturally candied honey. Many small producers have ruined electric mixers aerating honey this way!

As much as I love good honey, I don't use it a great deal in my cooking. I much prefer to spread it on a piece of toast or crusty, fresh, still-warm white bread with loads of unsalted butter. This is when I use my leatherwood or any other strongly flavoured honey such as imported Italian chestnut honey; these are also great poured over fresh ricotta. Every night I have a cup of hot milk flavoured with honey to help me sleep, but in this case I'm more likely to use a mild sugar-gum honey.

You often see honey used in cakes or puddings – Mrs Beeton gives a recipe for steamed honey pudding, which includes lemon rind and ginger and makes a delightfully comforting winter's treat.

When they were younger, my daughters loved chicken breasts that had been marinated with honey. Drizzle the chicken sparingly with honey, as if it were extra virgin olive oil, then add lots of chopped herbs and a squeeze of lemon juice and allow it to marinate for a good 30 minutes before baking at 180°C for 10–15 minutes, or grill it on the barbecue. Be careful that the chicken doesn't burn during cooking – if barbecuing, turn the chicken every minute or so to prevent this.

When I lived in Scotland and visited particular friends I was always given breakfast in bed on a beautifully set tray. Half a grapefruit was followed by a bowl of steaming porridge topped with a huge spoonful of honey almost as brown as treacle, and a big knob of butter that melted and oozed over the honey. It was marvellous.

A great tip from my honey supplier is to spray a small ceramic dish with a thin film of neutral-flavoured oil before filling it with honey to take to the breakfast table. The unused honey will then slip straight back into the jar.

If you can manage to substitute honey for sugar in a cake recipe (and it can't always be done), the cake will stay beautifully moist – if it lasts long enough in your household!

RICOTTA, HONEY AND PEARS   *Serves 12*

A whole round of ricotta surrounded by pears and drizzled with honey makes for a truly dramatic dessert, a new take on a cheese platter, or it works equally well as part of a Sunday brunch. I serve this on a raised cake stand, although you could use any large, round platter.

You'll need to visit a specialist cheese shop for the ricotta, and a rich, gutsy honey (not too sweet) really makes this dish special – try mallee, Manuka or leatherwood honey if you can find them. Or, to be totally indulgent, use imported chestnut honey.

3 ripe pears   **2 kg round pure whey handmade ricotta**
juice of ½ lemon   **(23 cm diameter)**
                                        400 ml honey

Slice the pears lengthways into thin slices and squeeze lemon juice over them so that they don't discolour, then arrange them around the ricotta. Drizzle the honey over the top, letting it run down the sides, and serve.

STEVE'S 'FROMAGE BLANC' WITH HONEYCOMB AND DESSERT WINE

Serves 4

This dish was served by Steve Flamsteed in his King River Café back in the late 1990s. It is a combination of an Alsatian dessert he used to eat during vintage in France, and one made by Steve Cumper, another friend and ex-employee of mine. The way it is eaten is as important as the dish itself. Steve Flamsteed writes, 'It's almost too many sensations but it works wonderfully!' Sometimes he reduces 750 ml of the dessert wine served with the dish to 100 ml, then stirs 2 tablespoons of this into the yoghurt 'cheese' instead of the honey.

Steve now combines his skills as wine-maker, chef and cheese-maker in his role at Giant Steps Winery in the Yarra Valley, where he is director of wine-making.

¼ cup (90 g) subtle honey (Salvation Jane or gum-blossom, for example)

500 g sheep's milk yoghurt

200 g honeycomb

8 almond biscotti

Australian dessert wine, to serve

Mix 1 tablespoon of the honey into the yoghurt, then tip this into a muslin-lined colander or sieve, place over a bowl and allow to drain overnight (you can do this on the kitchen bench if the weather is not too hot). The next morning the drained yoghurt or 'cheese' will be the consistency of mascarpone. Fold the remaining honey through the cheese and refrigerate it to enable you to form shapes for serving.

Using 2 dessertspoons, make quenelles by taking a spoonful of cheese, then using the other spoon to mould it into a smooth oval shape. Arrange 2 quenelles per person on serving plates alongside a square of fresh, dripping honeycomb and a couple of almond biscotti. Stand a macchiato glass of dessert wine on each plate.

To eat, dip the biscotti into the wine and then into the cheese. Any leftover cheese can be moved around the plate to soak up the honey that has dripped from the honeycomb. The final indulgence is to cleanse your palate by sucking any remaining honey from the honeycomb. Follow this with an espresso, which will melt any wax on your teeth!

STEPHANIE'S HONEY AND LAVENDER ICE CREAM

Makes 2 litres

My first taste of a lavender and honey ice cream was when renowned teacher and writer Madeleine Kamman visited Australia, a trip arranged by Di Holuigue of The French Kitchen, the iconic Melbourne cooking school. Madeleine added thyme and orange to hers, to great effect. This recipe comes from my friend Stephanie Alexander and is a great favourite. I like to serve it with an almond tart.

1 litre milk

1 cup lightly packed unsprayed lavender flowers

8 free-range egg yolks

330 ml honey

600 ml cream (45 per cent fat; see Glossary)

Bring the milk to the boil in a small saucepan, then pour it over the lavender in a bowl. Leave the lavender to infuse until the milk is cold.

Beat the egg yolks well, then beat in the honey. Strain the cold lavender milk into the honey mixture and beat gently to combine. Stir in the cream, then churn the mixture in an ice cream machine according to the manufacturer's instructions, and freeze.

KID

ONE OF THE REALLY IMPORTANT FOODS ON MY SPRING MENU in the restaurant days was kid. As with all game, kid (baby goat) is very healthy – low in fat and cholesterol. It is simple to prepare and quite delicious, and it is certainly encouraging to know that a wild resource is being used – feral goats are a pest in the Australian bush. Kid is now fairly widely available from Italian butchers, who often call it *capretto*.

With the exception of the Greek and Italian communities, kid is avoided by most Australians, yet this meat can be sweeter than lamb, with its own distinctive flavour, and is considered a delicacy in most Mediterranean countries.

In the restaurant days I had a local supplier, Rosemary Langley of Elm Tree Farm at Springton and, as I liked the meat so much myself, I had no difficulty getting people to try it. The goat was hung for a week in cold storage before cutting. It was basically cut in the same way as lamb, and as the animals were young (between 3 and 4 months) the shoulder, when braised whole, was my favourite cut.

Once again, our Saturday Barossa market is now my source for many things, amongst them kid – though, unless I ask, they tend to sell the older animals (more like 8–12 months). These are cooked quite differently, and the shoulder is best boned out and cubed for casseroles or curries, or stuffed and pot-roasted. The loins can be rubbed with preserved lemon pulp and lots of rosemary and bay leaves, then roasted. The legs can be roasted in exactly the same way, or in cooler weather, slow-roasted and basted with a mixture of port, extra virgin olive oil and chopped rosemary; otherwise, the boned meat can also be cubed for casseroles and curries.

The legs of the younger animal are marvellous pot-roasted slowly on a bed of ripe tomatoes and eggplant with loads of fresh herbs, or smeared with a paste of finely chopped mint, diced preserved lemon, extra virgin olive oil, sea salt flakes and freshly ground black pepper and wrapped in *crépine* (or caul fat, see Glossary).

It was Rosemary Langley who suggested to me that baking in an oven bag is an effective way to handle a leg of kid or goat. Her way was to rub it with extra virgin olive oil and garlic beforehand. Alternatively you could roast the leg at low temperature, basting it with a mixture of extra virgin olive oil, red wine, redcurrant jelly and honey, adding a tiny amount of water in the bottom of the roasting pan if it looked like burning.

Although I definitely prefer young kid, if it has had a good life an animal between 8 and 12 months old certainly has lots of flavour – and if well fed, it will also have some fat, so is perfect for roasting on a spit. Rosemary's son-in-law, Bronte Mawson, would often spit-roast such an animal and says that with salads and accompaniments, it could feed forty to fifty people. He would hire a spit oven rather like a large kettle barbecue. The advantage is that it has a lid and so, once stuffed, the animal does not need basting. The oven needs preheating for 30 minutes and then its even, slow heat will cook the kid in 2 hours. My addition to this would be to brush the skin with a mixture of either quince paste melted with a little lemon juice, or something as simple as a good bitter marmalade with sea salt flakes.

A more romantic version has the spit rigged over an open fire. This is more difficult to control because one needs to dig a pit and have sufficient coals for a 4-hour cooking period, and the spit has to be turned and the meat basted during this time. Baste with a mixture of verjuice and extra virgin olive oil – I would also add some garlic and rosemary.

I can imagine a baked whole kid served with native currant jelly. The first time I tried native currants, found in the Williamstown area in South Australia and a few other secret places, I was delighted by their sharp yet sweet flavour. (If they are picked under-ripe the tannin will dominate, so they should be avoided.)

While in Provence with Patricia Wells many years ago we visited her local butcher, Monsieur Henny, who delighted in showing us the food he was preparing for an evening party for friends. He took us upstairs via a steep spiral staircase to where there were cool-rooms and a kitchen with a huge oven that could accommodate an animal in one piece. That afternoon M. Henny had a baby kid cut into legs, shoulder and rack, which he marinated in a stainless steel roasting pan with olive oil, lemon rind, fine slices of lemon, finely chopped garlic and parsley; the head was also cut in half with the brain left in. M. Henny intended to roast the kid, let it rest in the roasting pan and then serve it with just the juices that accumulated around it.

I have braised all cuts of young kid, browned first with rosemary and then tossed into a saucepan with tomatoes (frozen from the summer crop at the peak of their flavour) and lots of onions and heads of garlic, turning frequently to ensure the juices don't burn. This takes 2–3 hours, even for such a young animal, because I cook it very slowly, using two simmer pads under the pot, sitting on the lowest possible flame. In the last 10 minutes of cooking, I throw in some black olives.

Another restaurant favourite was to pot-roast a cut of kid with a little vinegar, white wine, lemon, fresh bay leaves and oregano. During the slow-cooking the meat creates its own syrupy glaze – the trick is to have no more than 1 cm of liquid in the pan at any one time. Globe artichokes and eggplant are natural accompaniments.

Rub a leg of kid with coriander seeds (heat the seeds first in a dry frying pan and then pound them using a mortar and pestle to release their flavour) or chopped rosemary, extra virgin olive oil, salt and pepper. Brown the leg in a heavy-based roasting pan in a little more olive oil and then deglaze the pan with dry sherry. Chop up a base of onions, carrots and celery and place in the roasting pan; put the meat on top with some heads of garlic and a can of peeled tomatoes. Cook slowly in the oven at 160°C for 1½–2½ hours, until the meat is soft to the touch, and add more tomatoes if the liquid has evaporated. For the sauce, roast 4 heads of garlic in the oven and then squeeze out the garlic (the garlic will be wonderfully nutty and buttery, without the pungent taste of raw garlic). Pound a 45 g tin of anchovies, drained of oil, using a pestle and mortar, then add them to the garlic. Pour any pan juices from the kid into this mixture, stirring as if it were a mayonnaise.

Over the years, I have often either bought a single joint or a whole animal to cook on the spit or in our wood-fired oven. While not everyone is set up to cook a whole animal, it is not difficult to improvise a spit to cook a joint. A barbecue with a hood is another option, as is a kettle barbecue. If cooking a leg (although the preparation is much the same for a whole animal) in a kettle barbecue, first smother it with olive oil and your preferred herbs and flavourings – try oregano, freshly ground black pepper and slivers of garlic; fresh thyme and fennel seeds or rosemary and garlic; or lemon rind, slivers of garlic, fresh bay leaves and lots of chopped flat-leaf parsley. Cook the leg on a rack over a bed of chopped onion and ripe tomatoes at a lower temperature than you would, say, a leg of lamb, and only cook it for half as long. It's hard to give a precise cooking time, as so many variables apply, so cook until tender to the touch. The lower temperature is important no matter how small the animal is – goat dries out if exposed to high heat. As it is cooking, baste the kid with verjuice and red- or white-wine vinegar, with a little olive oil added if the leg seems to be drying out. Leave the meat to rest, covered, and away from the heat for a good 30 minutes after cooking, before carving.

If you don't have a kettle barbecue, a camp oven or cast-iron casserole with a tight-fitting lid placed on a simmer pad on the stovetop will do the trick beautifully. Cooked this way, the dish produces its own syrupy glaze – just make sure the tomato and onion are well moistened with olive oil.

Slow-cooking is perfect for late-night suppers or lazy lunches, especially when the days start to get a bit shorter and the air a bit nippier. So do give kid a try next time you pass an Italian butcher – you will be in for a treat.

ROAST SUCKLING KID *Serves 8–10*

This recipe is an old favourite inspired by Theodora Fitzgibbon's 1963 book, *Game Cooking*.

juice and finely grated rind of 1 lemon
1 suckling kid (about 5 kg)
500 g Granny Smith apples (about 3–4)
3–4 rashers streaky bacon, rind removed
3 sprigs rosemary
3 cloves garlic, peeled and sliced

1 tablespoon ground ginger
sea salt flakes and freshly ground
   black pepper
60 g butter
extra virgin olive oil, for roasting
285 ml cider

Preheat the oven to 180°C. Squeeze the lemon juice inside the kid and insert the lemon rind as well. Peel and core the apples and slice them thickly. Cut the bacon into 2.5 cm squares, render it in a dry pan, and then sauté the apple slices in the bacon fat with the rosemary. Make cuts in between the muscles of the leg and insert some of the apple slices, stuffing the rest into the cavity, using skewers where necessary to keep the slices in place.

Insert the garlic slices into the legs, mix together the ginger, salt, pepper and extra virgin olive oil, then rub this over the entire animal. Put into a roasting pan with the butter and some olive oil and roast for 20–30 minutes per kg (until tender to the touch), basting frequently. When it is cooked, remove the kid to a warm dish to rest for at least 30 minutes, pour off the surplus fat and add the cider to the pan juices. Boil rapidly over high heat on top of the stove until reduced by half, then pour over the kid before serving.

ELM TREE FARM'S STUFFING
FOR SPIT-ROASTED KID

Makes enough stuffing for one 8–12-month-old kid

breadcrumbs made from 2 loaves stale
    wood-fired bread
1 large onion, chopped
2 rashers bacon, chopped
2–3 cans pitted Morello cherries,
    drained and used whole
250 g pine nuts
250 g slivered almonds

150 ml white wine
150 ml homemade Plum Sauce
    (see page 70)
2 handfuls fresh flat-leaf parsley and
    marjoram, chopped
1 tablespoon coarsely ground black pepper
sea salt flakes

Mix together all the ingredients. The stuffing must be moist but not sloppy. Use to stuff a kid prepared for spit-roasting – it may be helpful to use an apple to hold the stuffing in place and stop it escaping during cooking.

CAFÉ C GOAT CURRY

Serves 12

For several years Mardie Palmer owned a tiny restaurant in Springton in the Valley called Café C. The food was simple and the place full of style; many Barossa stalwarts were regulars, and they loved this goat curry.

peanut oil, for cooking
4 onions, sliced
8 small red chillies, chopped (optional)
60 g fresh ginger, grated
4 cloves garlic, chopped
⅔ cup (200 g) red curry paste
2 kg diced goat

4 × 400 ml tins coconut milk
1.2 litres rainwater *or* spring water
20 kaffir lime leaves
juice of 4 limes
⅔ cup desiccated coconut, toasted
light soy sauce, to taste

Heat a little peanut oil in a large heavy-based saucepan over medium heat, then sauté the onions, chillies, ginger and garlic until onion is transparent – do not brown. Add the curry paste and fry gently for 3 minutes. Add the diced goat and stir until coated by the paste mixture. Increase the heat to high, then add the coconut milk, water, kaffir lime leaves and lime juice. Reduce the heat to low and simmer until tender. Stir in the toasted coconut and cook for another 5 minutes. Adjust seasonings to taste before serving.

LOQUATS

LOQUATS CAN, IN THE RIGHT CIRCUMSTANCES, BE A VERY welcome fruit. They are not much known or revered but it is their timing that, to me, makes them special. Arriving in November, which is an in-between time for fruit, they are, along with strawberries, the first hint that summer is to come. Oranges are past their peak, apples and pears are only from the cold store, so apart from the imported exotics, the loquat it is, at least until the first flush of raspberries starts to appear. The fruit has a distinctive flavour and is beautifully juicy.

The loquat is actually native to China and possibly the south of Japan, and I think it has a 'Japanese' look to it. The fruit is orange, oval, shiny and firm. There has not been much done to improve the genes of loquats in Australia and as far as I know they are only grown commercially in Japan and the Mediterranean, where they can easily grow to 5 cm long by 4 cm across. The Japanese have worked at improving the size, as the seeds of the loquat take up a large part of the fruit, and this seems to have been achieved without loss of flavour. I must confess I love the shiny, slippery feel of the seeds in my hand.

The South Australian climate certainly allows loquats to flourish, and many old-fashioned gardens contain huge specimens. The fruit marks easily yet the tree will respond to good care. What a delight it is to come across this evergreen tree with its wonderful large leaves, and boughs laden with fruit. My grandfather's garden in Sydney had a huge tree and as children we loved lying in its shade and eating the ripe fruit that had fallen to the ground, spitting out the shiny seeds as we ate.

Only two of the three loquat trees I planted survived, which is a real surprise, considering how hardy they are. The survivors are large lush trees and, together with a dozen maca-da-mia trees, provide year-round green screening from the road on our home property. The trick with loquats is to allow them to ripen enough to enjoy their juicy sweet flavour and that feeling of those shiny seeds rolling around your mouth. The birds love them too and as they don't ripen off the tree, it is a race to see who gets to enjoy the loquats first.

My dream of enclosing the loquat trees within a walled garden with 'weeder' geese to control the weeds just did not work, as the trees were on the wrong side of the house, and plans change as you spend time on a property. I simply transferred the idea of the geese to the quince orchard at the farm, although the fox problem there is still ever-present and I do not know what the long-term success of this will be.

With large loquats, it is worthwhile going to the trouble of quartering them, removing the seeds and poaching the fruit. (I only bother to peel them if the skins are marked, and then only once the fruit has been cooked.) Sprinkle the quartered fruit with sugar and then stand the saucepan over a gentle heat so the sugar starts to dissolve. Add enough sparkling wine to stop the fruit sticking and cook until the fruit has softened. Let the loquats cool, then serve with a dollop of cream, crème fraîche or mascarpone (depending on whether you delight in the slightly sour, as I do, or prefer something rich and sweet). Cooked in light sugar syrup with the addition of lemon to highlight their flavour, loquats make a lovely poached fruit to serve cold with fresh cream. They have a distinctive bitter-almond or marzipan flavour when poached.

APRICOT TART WITH CRÈME PÂTISSIÈRE
AND LOQUAT JELLY
Serves 8

Most apricot tart recipes will call for apricot jam for this, but I find the loquat jelly more subtle. Bake this tart in your favourite tart tin.

1 × quantity Sour-cream Pastry
   (see page 151)
2 tablespoons Loquat Jelly
   (see following page)

POACHED APRICOTS
1 cup (220 g) castor sugar
1 cup (250 ml) water
1 cup (250 ml) verjuice
20 apricots, halved and stoned

CRÈME PÂTISSIÈRE
2 cups (500 ml) milk
1 vanilla bean, halved lengthways
6 free-range egg yolks
70 g castor sugar
30 g flour
butter (optional), for cooking

Make and chill the pastry as instructed, then line a 20 cm tart tin with it. Chill the pastry case for 20 minutes. Preheat the oven to 200°C. Line the pastry case with foil, then cover with pastry weights and blind bake for 15 minutes. Remove the foil and weights and return the pastry case to the oven for a further 5 minutes or until golden brown.

To make the poached apricots, first make a syrup of the sugar, water and verjuice by heating them together until the sugar has dissolved (about 10 minutes). Gently poach the apricots in two batches in this syrup for 5–10 minutes, depending on their ripeness. Remove apricots from the syrup, and, when cool enough to handle, slip off their skins. »

To make the crème pâtissière, bring the milk to the boil in a saucepan, add the vanilla bean, then remove from the heat and allow it to infuse for 10 minutes. Whisk the egg yolks with the sugar until pale and the mixture forms a light ribbon. Sift in the flour and whisk again, then pour into a heavy-based saucepan. Strain the milk into the egg mixture, stirring constantly so no lumps form. Cook over a low yet direct heat, whisking constantly. Allow the mixture to come to the boil and simmer for a good 2 minutes to cook the flour. Add a tiny bit of butter at the last minute if you wish. Transfer the custard to a bowl to cool and place a piece of plastic film on the surface of the custard to prevent a skin forming.

Heat the loquat jelly in a small saucepan with a little water to thin it.

To assemble the dessert, fill the cooked pastry case with the crème pâtissière, then cover generously with the poached apricot halves, placed cut-side down. Brush the hot glaze over the apricots.

CARAMELISED LOQUATS   *Serves 10–12 as a dessert accompaniment*

The colour of this syrup is important: cook it until it is almost burnt or it will be too sweet. If you're worried about burning it, have a little cold water ready to add at the desired stage of caramelisation – but be warned, the mixture will splutter violently.

We would serve this at the restaurant, together with the Olive Oil and Sauternes Cake from Alice Waters' first book, *Chez Panisse Café Cookbook.* It is a cake I keep on using as a dessert in one guise or another; it is so moist it is almost a pudding, and it has a lovely lemony flavour.

> 1 kg large loquats, quartered and seeded   rind of 1 lemon, removed in one piece,
> 750 g castor sugar   if possible

Dry the loquats well with kitchen paper. Heat the sugar and 750 ml water in a shallow heavy-based saucepan (I use one with sides 12 cm high) over medium heat until the sugar dissolves and the syrup begins to change colour.

Gently slide the loquats and lemon rind into the pan and cook for a few minutes or until the loquats are soft but not pulpy. Transfer the fruit to a bowl with a slotted spoon, then continue cooking the syrup over medium heat until it becomes a deep-caramel colour. Let the syrup cool, remove the lemon rind and pour the caramel over the fruit (peeled, if you like).

LOQUAT JELLY

Loquats make a superior jelly for using as a glaze on fruit flans or tarts in the summer. The flavour of the loquat blends beautifully with the fruit rather than overpowering it. Crushing the cooked loquats to extract the juice gives off the most wonderful aroma, just like that of bitter almonds.

This recipe is adapted from one I found in Stephanie Alexander's book *Stephanie's Menus for Food Lovers* – I use a little less sugar and add lemon juice.

ripe loquats, roughly cut in half   **lemon juice, to taste**
sugar

Place the loquats in a heavy-based saucepan and add enough water to just cover the fruit. Bring to the boil and cook until the fruit is soft, approximately 15–20 minutes. Strain through a fine strainer, squeezing down on the fruit pulp to extract the juice, and discard the solids.

Measure out ¾ cup sugar for each cup juice and combine in a preserving pan. Taste the mixture, and add lemon juice if you find it too sweet. Bring to the boil and simmer until the jelly reaches setting point, skimming any scum off the surface as you go. To test, put a spoonful of jelly onto a saucer and cool in the refrigerator for a few minutes. If it wrinkles when you push it with your finger, the jelly is ready.

PEAS

THE BEST POSSIBLE PEA COMES DIRECT FROM THE GARDEN in the warmth of the afternoon. The sugar content of the pea picked this way is enough to satisfy the sweetest tooth. I'm sure any mother could persuade a recalcitrant child to eat greens like this. Who needs to cook greens anyway? Raw green peas – pods and all, if they are young enough – are a delight when eaten straight from the garden.

As peas grow older and larger, their sugar is converted into starch and they are not nearly as tasty. Few people bother shelling young peas. If you cannot buy young, freshly harvested peas then I'll go so far as to say that, in most cases, the ubiquitous frozen pea might even taste better. The sweetness of the pea is retained on freezing, but it is still a long way from the just-picked experience. Many of us have left behind the meat-and-three-veg principle (those old enough to have been brought up with it, I hasten to add), but I guess most people still rely on the convenience of frozen peas from time to time. For a quick fix, a green pea purée made from frozen peas can be a great accompaniment to a lamb chop, grilled fish, sweetbreads or lamb's fry.

Shelling peas is definitely a job to be shared around the kitchen table. As a child, I remember putting more in my mouth than in the pot. This never seemed to worry my mother – I'm sure she was a lot smarter about these things than me.

I wasn't aware until recently of how many varieties of pea there are. A close friend talked of eating telephone peas from her sister's garden in Tasmania – she called it one of life's sensuous pleasures. We have all become familiar with the snow pea or mangetout, which is picked for eating pod and all, with the peas inside hardly formed. This is lovely and crisp to eat raw or throw in salads, or to blanch for just a second and serve as a vegetable. The snow pea, along with the sugar snap pea (whose name says it all), has transformed the market for fresh peas. While more expensive than traditional peas, they keep their sweetness so much more than the normal pea. I can count on the fingers of one hand the

times that peas from my own garden have ended up in the pot – they're almost always eaten as they're picked. The same thing happens to a little delight called the asparagus pea, which looks like a delicate baby okra with frilled edges. For eating raw they should be picked when no more than 2 cm long. Not a vegetable you're likely to see flooding the market, but a nice one to grow for yourself. It really does have the characteristics of asparagus, with the sweetness of the pea, and is great as a crudité: you could serve it with a dish

of extra virgin olive oil, sea salt and freshly ground black pepper, or a rich garlic mayonnaise.

I have come to the conclusion that unless you grow peas yourself or buy them direct from growers' markets, they aren't worth the considerable trouble of shelling. The time between picking and buying them from a normal greengrocer is usually such that the sugars in the pea have all but vanished.

I once had a chef in my kitchen from the north of England and to him peas were mushy and accompanied fish and chips – all homemade, of course. He used dried peas which were soaked in a solution of bicarbonate of soda for four days. The peas were then washed and simmered in fresh water for 6–8 hours. When the peas were cooked to a mush, he added freshly ground black pepper, lots of butter and nutmeg.

Convenience foods are not necessarily bad, but nothing can compare with fresh produce in perfect condition, and this depends on seasonality and the distances involved in transporting produce to market. Years ago, I would cook fresh peas in just enough chicken stock to cover them, in a very small saucepan with a tight-fitting lid, adding a touch of sugar to compensate for the peas not coming fresh from the garden. Little cubes of butter and fresh mint were added at the last moment. I remember feeling very daring. Now my favourite way of serving fresh peas (those that make it to the saucepan) is to simmer them in a good stock until half done, then to finish cooking them in a little butter, salt and freshly ground black pepper. Throw in some prosciutto – the fatty parts particularly – just before finishing.

Should you be looking for reasons to shell and cook your own fresh peas (and I'd encourage you to do so, just to taste the difference), you don't need to look much further than Italian traditions. Angel hair pasta with fresh peas is one classic that's worth a look: poach peas and chopped leek in butter or extra virgin olive oil, then add fresh chervil and toss this through the just-cooked pasta. Or sauté the peas with chopped golden shallots over low heat and, when cooked, add strips of prosciutto or grilled pancetta and toss through the pasta.

So, what other dishes make peas worth the effort to shell? Pea mash, where fresh peas are simmered with golden shallots and butter until all the juice evaporates and the flesh mashes together, makes a lovely bed for a piece of grilled fish or great sausages. Then there is pea risotto, a dish I confess to making with dried Surprise peas out of season, on the advice of a good Italian cook, as they have a more intense flavour and are less likely to break up than frozen peas. Cook the base for the risotto in the same way as you would the pea mash and use a very delicate chicken stock to finish off the dish.

A soup worth the effort if you have just-picked peas to hand is chilled pea soup with buttermilk and chervil. First make a stock using the empty pea pods (but only if they are very fresh). Put half a chopped lettuce (iceberg will do fine), spring onions, celery, watercress (if you have it to hand) and chervil into the saucepan and just cover with water. Cook for about 30 minutes, then purée the mixture and press it through a colander to get rid of any fibrous matter. Sauté the shelled peas with some chopped leek over low heat for 10–15 minutes or until softened. Add the cooked peas and leek to the stock and purée with some buttermilk and fresh chervil to taste. This delicate and sweet soup is especially good chilled (as spring days can bring unexpected heat, cold soups can be very inviting). If you want to serve it hot, try adding a little cream instead of the buttermilk before heating gently.

The posthumous publication *The Enjoyment of Food: The Best of Jane Grigson* has a great recipe for a chilled soufflé of snow peas which I could imagine serving with some prosciutto, crusty bread and a glass of white wine for lunch.

PEAS WITH GOLDEN SHALLOTS *Serves 4 as an accompaniment*

When I first married I was given a book with a recipe for peas cooked 'the French way'. I used to think myself so clever when I had friends for dinner; the 1970s was definitely the dinner-party era when we all thought we had to show off. I remember how such a simple dish, given beautiful peas to start with, used to create such a stir, and I still love them today. This dish is based on that old recipe, with a couple of modern additions we would never have been able to get in the 1970s: golden shallots and sea salt flakes.

2 golden shallots, finely chopped	pinch sugar
3 tablespoons butter	pinch sea salt flakes
250 g fresh peas, shelled	¼ cup Golden Chicken Stock (see page 149)

In a heavy-based saucepan, sweat the golden shallots in the butter over gentle heat, then add the shelled peas and toss together. Season with the sugar and salt, and add enough stock to almost cover the mixture. Heat without bringing to the boil, then simmer, covered with a tight-fitting lid, over medium heat until the juices in the pan are all absorbed and the peas are cooked (this should take about 10 minutes for young peas, longer if they are older). This dish is a great accompaniment to lamb, chicken or fish.

FRESH PEA AND BUTTERMILK SOUP   *Serves 8*

The sweetness of the fresh peas contrasts beautifully with the sourness of the buttermilk in this dish.

2 onions, chopped	sea salt flakes
¼ cup extra virgin olive oil	1 litre vegetable stock
600 g fresh peas, shelled	1 cup buttermilk
½ bunch fresh chervil	white pepper, to taste

Soften the onion in the extra virgin olive oil until translucent. Add the peas and chervil, season with salt and pour in the vegetable stock. Bring to the boil over high heat, then turn heat down to medium and simmer, uncovered, for 8–10 minutes, until the peas are tender. Add buttermilk and bring back to a simmer. Transfer to a food processor, being careful not to overfill it or the heat will push the lid off, and purée until smooth. Season with white pepper, and serve warm with sprigs of fresh chervil.

SWEETBREADS WITH GREEN PEA PURÉE
AND GOLDEN SHALLOTS   *Serves 4*

1 kg oval-shaped sweetbreads (thymus gland if possible)	10 golden shallots, 4 thinly sliced and 6 peeled but left whole
juice of 2 lemons	butter, for cooking
1 fresh bay leaf	extra virgin olive oil, for cooking
1 kg fresh peas in pods	freshly ground black pepper
sugar, to taste	100 g prosciutto, cut into 4 cm × 2 cm pieces
sea salt flakes	

Soak the sweetbreads, replacing the water several times until no signs of blood remain. Place the cleaned sweetbreads in a saucepan with cold water, half the lemon juice and the bay leaf. Bring very slowly to a simmer, and remove the sweetbreads as they become opaque (about 3 minutes). Drain well and place on a flat dish with a similar-sized dish on top, then weight down with cans, or other weights, and leave in the fridge for 4 hours. Peel the sweetbreads of skin and gristle, keeping their shape intact.

Meanwhile, shell the peas, and blanch them twice in a saucepan of boiling water with a little sugar and salt added. (If you want the final purée to be very smooth, you may wish to blanch the peas for a third time.) In a saucepan over medium heat, sweat the chopped shallots in butter. Beginning with cold extra virgin olive oil in a cold frying pan (so they don't burn), caramelise the whole shallots over low heat until they are a gentle, golden brown and cooked all the way through. Purée the sliced shallots and peas while still warm, adding a little of the pea water, and season.

Slice the sweetbreads to desired size. Pan-fry them in nut-brown butter, with a dash of olive oil to prevent burning, until golden brown. Deglaze the pan with the remaining lemon juice, then toss in the prosciutto and add the caramelised shallots. Serve on a base of the green pea purée.

PASTA RAGS WITH SMALL GULF OR HARBOUR PRAWNS, FRESH PEAS AND CHERVIL
Serves 4

I often buy small prawns from my local market, where every second week a fisherman from the Spencer Gulf sells his catch. These prawns remind me of my childhood, when I would fish for prawns by lantern light in the shallows of Sydney Harbour at dusk. They are incredibly sweet and light years away from the larger prawn, often prized for its size rather than its flavour. What surprises me is that the quality of these prawns, as with those sold by Ferguson Fisheries in Adelaide, are such that even though they have already been cooked, I'm happy to peel them and toss them through the pasta right at the end, so the sweetness of the prawn and the pea are drawn together.

Pasta rags are square-shaped, and as such allow the sauce to adhere more readily.

1 × quantity Fresh Pasta (see page 152)	1 sprig chervil
2 tablespoons butter	¼ cup extra virgin olive oil
sea salt flakes	1 kg small gulf *or* harbour prawns
pinch sugar	fronds from 1 fennel bulb
125 g fresh peas, shelled	freshly ground black pepper

Make, chill, and roll the pasta as instructed, then cut it into rags (I tend to cut mine on the slant into 5 cm squares) and spread out on clean tea towels until required. This prevents the pasta rags from sticking together or drying out too fast. If it will be a while before you start cooking, dampen the tea towels (don't leave it longer than about an hour, though – the pasta is best cooked soon after making).

In a small saucepan, add around ½ cup water (or enough to cover the base to just over 1 cm), and add 1 tablespoon of the butter, a pinch of sea salt and a pinch of sugar. Bring to a simmer, then add the peas and a sprig of chervil and cover the pan with a tight-fitting lid. Cook for 10 minutes, or until the peas are tender. Strain off the juices, then add the other tablespoon of butter and stir through.

Cook the pasta rags in boiling salted water. This should take 2–4 minutes after the water has come to the boil, depending on how fine the pasta has been rolled.

Drain the pasta, reserving a tablespoon or two of cooking liquid in case you want to moisten the completed dish. Add the extra virgin olive oil, prawns and peas to the pasta and toss together to heat the prawns through. Check for seasoning and serve with fennel fronds scattered over.

POTATOES

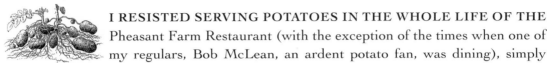

I RESISTED SERVING POTATOES IN THE WHOLE LIFE OF THE
Pheasant Farm Restaurant (with the exception of the times when one of
my regulars, Bob McLean, an ardent potato fan, was dining), simply
because my childhood had a surfeit of them and, I have to admit, they just didn't excite me.
That is, until the arrival of the waxy potato – what a change that made to my cooking.
When made with waxy potatoes, I finally grew to love the mashed potato that my husband
Colin likes to cook (one in his small repertoire of dishes). Most feel that waxy potatoes are
ideal for boiling but not mashing, however I love waxies mashed (or 'smashed') with lots of
unsalted butter or extra virgin olive oil. I now only make my gnocchi with waxy potatoes
– any variety, from desiree to pink-eyes – and have found they add a whole new dimension.
At times I just boil waxy potatoes, let them cool a little, then cut them in half and toss them
in extra virgin olive oil with some rinsed salted capers and lots of flat-leaf parsley. Potatoes
are one ingredient that I have changed my mind about completely, and now I love to use
the waxy varieties in many different ways.

I had been spoilt: in my early twenties I lived on the Isle of Skye in Scotland and experienced the joys of potatoes grown in the paddock between the house and the sea. Seaweed
was pulled up over the patch as mulch, and we'd dig up the potatoes as we needed them.
No potato available to me here has ever reached the heights of these Scottish 'tatties'. It was
not unusual to have a meal just of potatoes boiled and literally smothered in locally made
butter. I can still taste them as I write, so similar to the iron-like tang of a fresh oyster, and
it reminds me what a simple life it was.

Whilst in Scotland, I even learnt to cut peat for the fire and to make haggis in the
kitchen sink. On reflection, it was here that my interest in game began (to tell the truth,
I suspect our game was come by more from poaching than via any toff's estate shooting
party). I quickly learnt of the abundance of wild produce: cockles collected from the shore;
the salmon offered by a neighbour. Once, while fishing in a tiny row boat (only metres

from the front paddock where we had spent the day stooking hay), my companion spent his whole time extracting the fish from my hooks and baiting them again. (I also have memories of rowing the boat to another island under a full moon in search of something that I can no longer recall – through lack of skill, our expeditions were often more fanciful than fruitful.) And when we were too tired to cook, it was back to potatoes again. It was

an idyllic life, and one I was almost tempted to make my own for a time.

The waxy potatoes now available are, I feel, as close as I'll ever come to the perfection I enjoyed on Skye. They have a dense texture and a pronounced flavour, even without butter or olive oil. There has been a veritable deluge of new varieties, and a significant amount of research on these has been undertaken within Australia in recent years. The revolution has begun!

My favourite waxy variety of all is the Tasmanian pink-eye from the shaly soil south of Hobart. Pink-eyes (often marketed as Southern Gold potatoes on the mainland) are first ready for market near Christmas time, when you can eat them just picked, so young that the skins rub off in your fingers before cooking; I love them with loads of unsalted butter, and a meal of these alone is a feast. Now while I admit that this waxy variety is considered too dry to mash by most, I love the flavour so much that I do it anyway (I just add lots of butter or good extra virgin olive oil to ensure a moist result, leaving out the cream), and the result is delicious.

After these, I probably prefer kipfler (best boiled or steamed, although they are also good slow-baked whole in casseroles), pink fir apple potatoes and Dutch creams. Next in line would be bintje, nicola and patrone, which are excellent boiled for use in salads. The first and most readily available waxy potato was the desiree, a Dutch potato with a dark-pink skin and yellow flesh; I love it both boiled and mashed. When small, desirees are good for potato salads or roasting. Spunta, another Dutch variety, has a creamy-white skin and yellow flesh and is great for chipping. I never make gnocchi without the best waxies I can find, nor do I make a potato salad, warm or chilled, with anything else. It's waxies for me every time, which I know goes against the usual wisdom.

The irony is that the really delicious pink-eye has been grown in small pockets across Tasmania since about the late 1800s, when it is thought to have been introduced from the Canary Islands. At first it was grown quite specifically in black sandy dunes laden with shell grit at Seacroft in the south, land that would seem inhospitable to anything else. Perhaps there is something in the flavour of these potatoes grown so close to the sea that brings back memories of those I enjoyed on Skye.

I have also heard wonderful stories about an enterprising potato farmer who took the pink-eye to the heavier soils in Tasmania's north-west, the traditional potato belt. Apparently he made a killing on the Melbourne market during the 1956 Olympics, as chefs paid him a king's ransom for what were possibly the first waxy potatoes ever eaten on the mainland.

Traditionalists feel that black sandy soils give the best flavour of all, but opinion is divided. To me, the point here is that true regional differences should be celebrated. Whatever these are, in both the north and south of Tasmania, the best of the pink-eyes are planted so as to be ready for Christmas Day, when the flesh is at its yellowest and waxiest. And the most delicious of these new season's pink-eyes are the chats, left behind by traditional farmers – tiny round potatoes little more than a couple of centimetres across, and sweeter than you can imagine.

Fresh pink-eyes react badly to the fluorescent lights used in supermarkets, so need to be sealed in very thick brown paper bags and sold quickly. Grown for generations at his family's property 'Seacroft' in South Arm, in the traditionally favoured black sandy soil, John Calvert's pink-eyes are sold this way by renowned providore Wursthaus in Hobart, with the history of the farm written on the bag.

With the right potatoes, a dish can go from average to exceptional. Sitting in glorious late-winter sunshine at Bistro Moncur in Sydney some years ago, where my friend Damien Pignolet – a great chef and teacher and an absolute perfectionist – continually inspires me, I ate a warm salad of waxy potatoes with sorrel, soft-boiled egg and oil (was it olive or walnut?). The combination of first-class ingredients and the skill of the kitchen made the dish quite perfect, yet it wouldn't have reached the same heights if the potatoes used hadn't been waxy. With some good crusty bread and a glass of bubbles, it was all I could want, and the perfect antidote to exhaustion.

If you don't have easy access to a good range of waxy potatoes, simply search out the variety you want, let them go to seed, then plant them. I arrange them in neat rows because it is only when the plant dies back that the potatoes are ready to 'bandicoot' for, and I need good markers so I don't rip up the whole garden in my frenzy to find the buried treasure.

For those not as enamoured of waxy potatoes, the most readily available non-waxy potatoes are the coliban, sebago, pontiac and kennebec. The round, red-skinned pontiac is an all-purpose potato that is good boiled, mashed or roasted. I used to prefer small pontiacs and almost never peeled them for roasting or boiling. The coliban, a purple-blushed white potato, is round with white flesh. It breaks up when boiled but is not bad for roasting and is quite good for chips. While deemed an all-rounder, the oval, white sebago, which has white flesh, is best mashed. Another all-rounder, the large, white-skinned, white-fleshed kennebec is excellent for chips. The best variety of all for chips is the russet burbank, but this is rarely available commercially, since McDonald's buy it almost exclusively.

As staple a vegetable as the potato is, you would think that we would have learnt how to store it properly. But the increased use of plastic bags and fluorescent lights has meant we're further away from getting it right than ever: plastic makes potatoes sweat and causes them to deteriorate quickly, while exposure to light makes them develop bitter green patches that, at worst, can cause illness when eaten. Your best bet is to buy loose, unwashed potatoes in a brown paper bag. Avoid those with green patches (although the green can be cut away), cuts, cracks, bruises, wet patches or a musty smell.

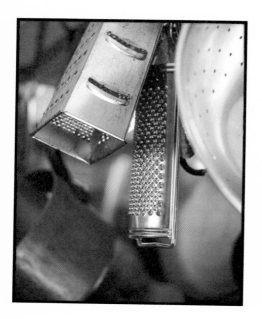

If you have succumbed to convenience and bought potatoes in a plastic bag, remove them from the bag as soon as you arrive home. Store the potatoes in a cool, dark place with good ventilation – do not refrigerate them. Do not scrub unwashed potatoes until ready to use them, as this will hasten deterioration (it is worth noting here that unwashed potatoes last longer than washed potatoes). I delight in finding potatoes just going to seed at the back of my cupboard: the starch of these old spuds has broken down and they are wonderfully sweet – my friend Stephanie thinks I'm crazy to like these. I only throw them away if they're green. If you've found similar potatoes but think they're sprouting too much to eat, plant them so that you will have your own potatoes to dig on demand.

You need do very little to good-quality, flavoursome potatoes – but that doesn't mean they don't go well with exotic ingredients. Try something as indulgent as potatoes with caviar. Boil 500 g unpeeled waxy potatoes in salted water for 15–20 minutes or until cooked through (different varieties need different cooking times). While the potatoes are still hot, scoop out about half the flesh and either mash it or put it through a food mill or potato ricer. Allow a couple of knobs of butter to melt into the hot mashed potato, then stir in 150 ml crème fraîche and season with salt and freshly ground black pepper. Pile the mixture back into the potatoes and add a generous tablespoon of salmon roe or caviar to each. A small potato cake made from butter-fried mashed potato and topped with crème fraîche, fresh oysters and caviar is another way of combining these flavours. For me, it's important to bite into the oyster rather than just swallow it – it gives me that iron-like flavour I crave in the potato.

Another extravagant combination is to shave a fresh truffle over a salad of warm baby waxy potatoes drizzled with extra virgin olive oil and seasoned with sea salt flakes and freshly ground black pepper. This is all pretty powerful stuff, but the potato has the strength not to be drowned out.

Roast potato takes on a new meaning when you toss thickly sliced unpeeled potato with olive oil and intersperse it in a baking dish with thick slices of meyer lemon and sprigs of thyme. Drizzle over some extra virgin olive oil and season with salt and freshly ground black pepper, then bake at 200°C for about 45 minutes until the potato is soft, the lemon caramelised and the edges a little charred.

Potatoes are wonderful cooked in goose or duck fat left over from making confit. Cut 500 g potatoes into 5 mm-thick slices, then seal the slices on both sides in 125 ml fat in a 200°C oven. Turn the heat down to 180°C and allow the potato to cook through. A sprig of fresh rosemary or thyme is great added to the pan when sealing the potato slices.

Cook potato this way if you have freshly gathered young pine mushrooms, but use nut-brown butter with a dash of extra virgin olive oil rather than goose or duck fat. Seal the mushrooms the same way as you do the potato, but use a separate frying pan and only cook them for 3–5 minutes. I would use basil or thyme with the mushrooms, and might even add finely diced golden shallots. The mushrooms will give off lovely juices as they rest. As soon as the potato is done, toss it with the mushrooms, then season the dish and serve it as a meal on its own, or as a side dish to pan-fried veal chops; deglaze the veal pan with a little lemon juice to make a sauce.

Colin claims to make the best mashed spuds in the world, and I wouldn't dream of interfering, as I'm happy whenever he wants to cook anything for me. He almost always uses lashings of butter and cream (but not too much so it goes runny), and sometimes he uses the best extra virgin olive oil, lots of sea salt flakes and freshly ground black pepper. The ingredient that is always constant, though, is finely chopped onion – and he always uses only part of an onion, then wraps the rest and puts it carefully in the fridge, only to find the next time he looks that I have thrown it out, as I can't bear the odour of onion permeating the rest of the food in the fridge. Old habits die hard!

Both Saskia and Elli grew up in a household almost devoid of potatoes, due to my early prejudice against them, and unless their dad was showing off his mashed spuds, we almost never ate them. (Should I confess now that I hardly ever gave them a baked dinner either? They'd tell me they were deprived!) But times have changed. I have been known to get more excited about presenting a dish of freshly dug pink fir apple potatoes, some of them full-sized and some like tiny little nuggets, or at Christmastime a dish of pink-eyes from the markets, than a three- or four-course feast. Simply boiled and drained, then served with some very green extra virgin olive oil (although you could well use lots of butter instead), a good sprinkling of sea salt flakes and freshly ground black pepper, we devour them with gusto. When the mood is right, nothing else is needed for dinner.

BEST ROAST POTATOES WITH
PRESERVED LEMON AND ROSEMARY

Serves 4–6

For this recipe I'd choose desirees or pontiacs if waxy potatoes are not available, as they are great when roasted.

2 kg best in-season potatoes

1 cup (250 ml) extra virgin olive oil

2 quarters preserved lemon, flesh removed, rind rinsed and cut into strips

sea salt flakes and freshly ground black pepper

2 sprigs rosemary

Preheat the oven to 180°C. Peel the potatoes or wash the skins, then cut into quarters. Place in a roasting pan and coat with the olive oil, lemon strips, salt and pepper. Roast the potatoes for 45 minutes, stirring occasionally to make sure they do not stick to the pan. Sprinkle on the rosemary and cook for another 10 minutes or until potatoes are crisp and cooked through, then serve immediately.

ROAST WAXY POTATOES WITH PANCETTA, CAPERS AND PRESERVED LEMON

Serves 4

250 g kipflers *or* other waxy potatoes, washed, dried and halved lengthways

½ preserved lemon, flesh removed, rind rinsed and thinly sliced

4 thin slices flat pancetta

50 ml extra virgin olive oil

freshly ground black pepper

2 teaspoons capers

1 tablespoon chopped flat-leaf parsley

sea salt flakes

Preheat the oven to 220°C. Toss the potatoes with the preserved lemon, pancetta, olive oil and some pepper in a large, shallow, heavy-based roasting pan. If the pan is too crowded, it is better to divide the ingredients between two pans so that the potatoes caramelise and the pancetta crisps, as they will stew rather than bake in a crowded pan.

Bake for 20–35 minutes or until golden; the exact time will depend on the variety of potato and oven used. Shake the pan to loosen the contents, then add capers and flat-leaf parsley, season to taste and serve immediately.

WARM SALAD OF WAXY POTATOES AND BEANS

Serves 6–8

2 cups (200 g) shelled walnuts

½ cup (125 ml) good quality walnut oil

2 tablespoons verjuice

generous squeeze of lemon juice

2 tablespoons cream

sea salt flakes and freshly ground black pepper

500 g baby green beans

500 g small waxy potatoes

Preheat the oven to 220°C. Dry-roast the walnuts on a baking tray for 6–8 minutes, then rub off the skins with a tea towel and sieve away any remaining bitter skin (new season's walnuts will not require this).

Make a vinaigrette by mixing the walnut oil, verjuice and lemon juice, then add the cream, season and set aside. Trim the beans if necessary. Put two saucepans of salted water on to boil.

Boil the potatoes in one pan for about 15 minutes until cooked, then drain immediately. Cook the beans in the other pan for 5 minutes so they are still a little al dente. Drain the beans and allow them to cool a little. Toss the potatoes with the vinaigrette, beans and walnuts and serve immediately.

GNOCCHI WITH CRISP SAGE LEAVES   *Serves 6–8*

I love all things Italian, and gnocchi particularly. Success in making it always eluded me until I compared the results I got from using melted butter versus egg, and using kneaded versus un-kneaded dough. This recipe is now my preferred way of making gnocchi as it results in substantial, earthy, yet not heavy gnocchi, rather than the light-as-air variety. But this is a case of 'horses for courses', and if I was serving gnocchi with something delicate I'd probably do it differently to this. This dish is perfect as a first course or, without the sage leaves, makes an excellent side dish for a juicy braise.

1⅓ cups (200 g) plain flour	freshly ground black pepper
500 g waxy potatoes	handful sage leaves
salt	extra virgin olive oil, for cooking
175 g unsalted butter	Parmigiano Reggiano, to serve

Spread the flour out into a rectangle on your work surface. Peel the potatoes if you wish, then steam them for 15 minutes or until cooked through. While hot, pass each potato through a potato ricer and let it fall evenly over the flour on the bench. Sprinkle with salt.

Preheat the oven to 180°C. Melt 50 g of the butter and drizzle it evenly over the potato. Work the flour into the potato little by little using a pastry scraper until you have a firm dough. Knead the dough gently for a few minutes. Divide the dough into quarters and roll each piece to make a long thin sausage about 1 cm in diameter. Cut each sausage into 2.5 cm lengths. Put a buttered serving dish into the oven.

I find a large, heavy-based, 6 cm-deep roasting pan perfect for poaching gnocchi. Fill the tin with water, then salt it and bring it to the boil over medium heat. When the water is boiling, increase the heat to high and quickly slip in all the gnocchi at once (if the dish is large enough to take the gnocchi in a single layer), then reduce the heat to medium so the water isn't too turbulent. Allow the gnocchi to cook for 1 minute after they have risen to the surface, then skim them out, put them into the warm serving dish and season. Return the dish to the oven to keep warm while you crisp the sage.

Cook the sage leaves in a frying pan in the remaining butter and a dash of olive oil over medium heat until the butter is nut-brown and the sage crisp. It is important that the sage leaves become crisp without the butter burning. Pour the butter and sage over the hot gnocchi and serve immediately with shaved Parmigiano Reggiano on the table.

QUANDONGS

ABORIGINAL AUSTRALIANS TREASURED THE QUANDONG AND ATE the fruit raw or dried it for later use; it was a valuable source of vitamin C. In *Bush Food*, Jennifer Isaacs describes how Aborigines burnt the branches of the quandong tree and stood their children in the smoke in order to make them strong for long journeys. A tea was also made from quandong leaves and drunk as a purgative, and an infusion made from the roots of the tree was believed to help rheumatism sufferers. The bark was used for tanning leather and the wood was also of value, being closely related to sandalwood.

The first stanza of 'The Quandong Tree', a poem by Mary Flyn that appeared in the *Australian Women's Mirror* some forty years ago, reflects the ever-present nature of the tree in outback Australia:

> *In childhood books I read of these –*
> *Cherry and quince and walnut trees*
> *And many another old-world tree.*
> *Exotic and far they seemed to be,*
> *For all there was, my dears, for me,*
> *Was just one little quandong tree.*

The quandong evokes fond memories for people in the outback – childhood memories of gathering wild quandongs, eating quandong pies, and making necklaces out of the seeds.

The quandong tree will survive in the harshest of conditions and will cope with an amazingly high level of salinity, making quandongs a perfect desert-climate fruit. There are growers and CSIRO researchers working together on finding a way to propagate this fruit that is economically viable. Although there have been some successes, there is still a great deal to be done before the quandong can become more widely accessible.

While I have heard the taste of fresh quandongs described as somewhere between peach and rhubarb with a piquancy that makes your mouth pucker, I have not yet tried them myself. Once some were sent to me through the mail, but they did not survive the journey. Frozen quandongs are now available through Outback Pride Fresh in 1 kg packs and are a wonderful addition particularly when cooking game.

I really like the flavour of dried quandongs, although I've experienced huge variation in quality. It is a fruit that can be used for both savoury and sweet dishes. The only time I tasted a commercially made quandong pie, in the Flinders Ranges, I felt that too much sugar had been added and this masked the unique flavour. I have since been told by many people that it is better to use honey as a sweetener as this is less likely to mask the original flavour.

At the Pheasant Farm Restaurant, I used to team dried quandong with venison and kangaroo, finding the intense bittersweet flavour a great foil for the rich meat. In my quest to use local produce in as many ways as possible, I made a dessert of quandongs in a bread-and-butter pudding. As well as using quandongs in the pudding itself, I reconstituted some and served them in a caramel, making sure the caramel was almost bitter so that the natural sweet–sour flavour wasn't overpowered by too much sugar.

QUANDONG, MACADAMIA AND CHOCOLATE TART
Serves 10

50 g dried quandongs

1 cup (250 ml) verjuice

1 × quantity Sour-cream Pastry
   (see page 151)

300 g sugar

250 g unsalted butter

250 g raw unsalted macadamias,
   roughly chopped

5 free-range eggs, at room
   temperature, beaten

80 g Haigh's bitter couverture chocolate
   (see Glossary)

Soak the quandongs in the verjuice overnight.

The next day, preheat the oven to 200°C. Make and chill the pastry as instructed, then roll it out and use to line a greased 26 cm tart tin. Trim the edges. Line the pastry case with foil, cover with pastry weights and blind bake for 15 minutes. Remove the foil and pastry weights and bake for another 5 minutes.

For the filling, dissolve 150 g of the sugar in 150 ml water in a saucepan, simmer for 5 minutes then gently poach the quandongs in this sugar syrup, along with any remaining verjuice, until tender. This should take approximately 20 minutes but will vary depending on how dried the quandongs were. Remove the fruit from the pan, then increase heat to high and boil the cooking liquid until it reduces to a syrup, then set aside.

To make the macadamia filling, combine the butter and macadamias in a food processor, then slowly add the eggs and the remaining sugar with the motor running.

Arrange the cooked quandongs over the pastry base, grate over the chocolate, then spread with the macadamia mix. Return to the oven and bake for 20 minutes or until golden. While the tart is still warm, pour over the reduced syrup.

QUANDONG JAM   *Makes about 1.5 litres*

This recipe was inspired by one given to me by Jenny Treeby of CSIRO, using fresh quandongs. It is wonderful to see a researcher taking a real interest in the end product – the preserving of the fruit.

As dried quandongs are easier to find than fresh, I have adapted the recipe accordingly.

250 g dried quandongs   800 g sugar
100 ml lemon juice

Reconstitute the dried quandongs in 1 litre of water overnight. Place the soaked fruit and its soaking water, the lemon juice and 500 ml water in a large, heavy-based saucepan and simmer over medium–high heat for 20 minutes, then add the sugar. Turn the heat to low and simmer until jam reaches setting point (about 1½ hours). To test, put a spoonful of jam onto a saucer and cool in the refrigerator for a few minutes. If it wrinkles when you push it with your finger, the jam is ready. Transfer to sterilised glass jars (see Glossary).

SNAPPER

IT SEEMS I HAVE SPELT SNAPPER INCORRECTLY ALL MY LIFE.
I understood 'schnapper' to be the European spelling of the same fish, but I now find that our snapper is actually a different fish from the European schnapper, although they superficially resemble one another. The European schnapper is low-yielding and relatively inexpensive, whereas our snapper is a lot fleshier, and is thought by many to be the best-tasting snapper in the world.

The diet of the snapper includes crabs, squid, sea urchins and mussels. As many blue swimmer crabs in South Australia moult and lose their shells between full moons in November and December, it makes sense that spring is probably the peak time to eat local snapper, making it the exception to the rule that fish are best in winter.

Over the years, my information about fish has come from such luminaries as John Sussman, ex-Flying Squid Brothers and, in my mind, the foremost expert on fish in the country, and Kim Rogers, formerly of International Oysters of Adelaide, both of whom have been responsible for educating cooks and fishermen alike throughout Australia for the last decade or more. In my lifetime the quality of Australian fish has increased dramatically, from the way it is caught to the way it is brought to market. People like John and Kim, who are concerned about quality and flavour, and the various fisheries departments, which focus on research and development, are all vital links in the chain.

Snapper is found along most of the southern coast of Australia, from inshore waters to a depth of 100 metres. At times they can be seen in large schools of up to 30 tonnes in relatively shallow waters, where they tend to gather around natural or artificial reefs to spawn. There is a tendency for snapper to move into deeper waters as they get older, where they stay until they are twelve or thirteen years of age, before returning to inshore waters for the remainder of their lives. Snapper reach legal size (38 cm) at six years of age, when they weigh a bit less than a kilogram. These young snappers are known as 'ruggers' to fishermen but are usually called 'baby snapper' in the market. They are the best prize of all – the flesh is close, firm and at its sweetest. The bigger the fish, the bigger the flakes, making the flesh easier to separate. 'Nobbers' weighing around 10 kg can be up to thirty-five years old.

Snapper is definitely high on the list of my favourite fish, but then given the right conditions, flathead and King George whiting are truly exceptional, and the sashimi of southern bluefin tuna I have eaten in Japan is, at its best, nothing short of sensational. However, with any fish it is all about the quality that is available to you – and I think snapper is the best readily available fish you can buy. It is not cheap and, with such a large head (and gut cavity), snapper does not have a great deal of flesh, but it is still worth every cent. The heads make the best fish stock. Buying cutlets is the most economical way to purchase snapper, and a kilogram will feed five people exceptionally well for a main course.

There are lots of options for cooking snapper, but my favourites are the simplest. A well-seasoned fillet or cutlet (as my friend Michael Angelakis, South Australia's largest fish merchant, says, 'If it comes from the sea it needs salt!') seared in nut-brown butter for as little as 2–3 minutes a side, depending on its thickness, and finished with lots of freshly ground black pepper and a good splash of verjuice or a squeeze of lemon is all I need to be happy.

Snapper and oysters have a great affinity – it's that saltiness again, along with the combination of textures, that works so well. Reduce Fish Stock (see page 98) with a little champagne, then stir in some warm cream that has been infused with saffron threads and reduce the sauce further. Add the oysters and serve immediately with snapper that has been pan-fried or brushed with extra virgin olive oil and baked.

There is not a great deal of difference in the time it takes to bake whole snapper of varying weights: a fish that weighs 1 kg will take 20–25 minutes at 200°C, while a 3 kg fish might take 35–40 minutes. (A 1 kg snapper will feed two or three people, and a 3 kg fish will feed six to eight.) As overcooked fish is a travesty, don't compute minutes for kilograms, as you would for meat. However, as with meat and poultry, you should allow the fish to rest after it has been cooked to ensure moistness.

Snapper can withstand robust Mediterranean flavours in a stuffing, such as olives, capers, anchovies or preserved lemons with lots of flat-leaf parsley or basil. The main thing is to cook with ingredients to hand and not think you have to follow recipes slavishly. When Colin came home from the market with a whole snapper recently I mixed together chopped flat-leaf parsley, anchovies, olives and slices of meyer lemon (all of which I had in my pantry and garden), along with chunky roasted breadcrumbs, then seasoned the mixture and packed it into the fish before baking it. If you have snapper cutlets and want a quick and easy meal, butter a piece of foil or baking paper large enough to wrap a cutlet, then position the fish on it and pack on a layer of this lemon mixture. Close up the parcels and bake them at 200°C for about 7 minutes. Slide the fish and its 'stuffing' straight onto serving plates – the juices make a wonderful sauce – and drizzle with some more extra virgin olive oil.

SNAPPER WITH AVOCADO AND TOMATO SALSA   *Serves 6*

Whenever I serve raw fish I offer a vinaigrette in a separate jug for those who want it, as the lemon juice or other acidulant in the vinaigrette actually 'cooks' the raw fish – and I prefer my fish totally raw. Once, when I was in Sydney for a conference, I revelled in a dish of raw tuna at Neil Perry's Mars Bistro in Rushcutters Bay. Based on a salade niçoise, the dish had slices of just-cooked waxy potatoes at the base, stacked with a pile of cooked tiny green beans, quarters of peeled and seeded tomatoes, the smallest capers and green olives and a delicate vinaigrette. Right on top lay four large rosy-pink slices of raw tuna in perfect condition, overlapping like roof tiles and totally 'undressed'. It was as close to perfection as you could get!

But raw isn't everyone's bag, so if you prefer your fish cooked, then try the following. Save all your energy for finding a really good seafood merchant; the actual cooking of the fish is the easy part.

6 snapper fillets	SALSA
extra virgin olive oil, for cooking	1 large avocado, diced
6 quarters preserved lemon, flesh removed, rind rinsed and cut into strips	2 vine-ripened tomatoes, diced
freshly ground black pepper	1 small red onion, diced
butter, for cooking	verjuice *or* lemon juice, to taste
sea salt flakes	sea salt flakes and freshly ground black pepper
¼ cup (60 ml) verjuice	2 tablespoons flat-leaf parsley, roughly chopped
⅓ cup chopped flat-leaf parsley	extra virgin olive oil, for drizzling

Toss the fish with a little olive oil, the preserved lemon and some pepper. Set aside.

For the salsa, mix the avocado, tomato and onion, then add a dash of verjuice or a good squeeze of lemon juice to taste, season with salt and pepper and add the parsley and a little olive oil to combine.

In a large frying pan, melt 3 tablespoons butter and heat over medium–high heat until it turns nut-brown. Immediately add a dash of oil to save it from burning. Season the fillets with salt and cook the first side over medium–high heat with the preserved lemon, until the surface is sealed and lightly caramelised from the butter, then turn the fillets over and cook just until they become opaque, which takes minutes only.

Remove the cooked fish and lemon from the pan and reserve, then add the verjuice and reduce it quickly over high heat. Remove the pan from the heat and swirl in extra virgin olive oil to taste to make a warm vinaigrette, then add the parsley.

Serve the snapper fillets with the pan juices poured over, and some avocado and tomato salsa alongside.

SNAPPER IN A PARCEL

Serves 4

Serving fish *en papillote* is a breeze, and it means that you can create any number of different sauces by just adding a few flavourings to the parcel before cooking: a little butter, cream, extra virgin olive oil, wine, fresh herbs, slices of meyer lemon or a dash of lemon or lime juice, in whatever combination takes your fancy. Salmon fillets or cutlets are also delicious when treated this way.

extra virgin olive oil, for cooking

1 small fennel bulb, trimmed and sliced, fronds reserved

4 × 200 g snapper fillets of equal thickness, skin removed

1 meyer lemon, sliced

handful fresh chervil sprigs *or* bay leaves, optional

sea salt flakes and freshly ground black pepper

Heat a little extra virgin olive oil in a frying pan, then sauté the fennel over medium heat until cooked through.

Preheat the oven to 200°C. Liberally oil 4 sheets of baking paper or foil large enough to wrap the fish fillets. Arrange the cooked fennel and reserved fronds on the paper as a bed for the fish. Position the fillets on top, then add the lemon slices, followed by the chervil or bay leaves if using. Drizzle with extra virgin olive oil, then season and carefully fold in the edges to seal the parcel. Transfer the parcels to a baking tray (a scone tray is ideal for this) and bake for 8 minutes. Let the fish rest for another 5 minutes before serving.

When everyone opens their parcels they will be surrounded by a wonderful aroma as the juices spill onto the plate. Drizzle over a little more extra virgin olive oil, add a boiled waxy spud and a green vegie or salad and your meal is complete.

SNAPPER WITH SORREL AND PANCETTA

Serves 2–3

3 thick slices white bread, crusts removed and cut into large cubes

extra virgin olive oil, for cooking

1 very large onion, finely chopped

1 sprig thyme

8 thin slices mild pancetta, cut into strips

8 sorrel leaves

sea salt flakes and freshly ground black pepper

1 × 1 kg snapper

1 lemon

Preheat the oven to 200°C. Place the bread cubes on a baking tray, drizzle with a little of the olive oil and bake until golden brown. Allow the bread to cool, then process in a food processor – you will need ¾ cup breadcrumbs. Reset the oven temperature to 220°C.

Gently sweat the onion and thyme in a frying pan in a little olive oil until the onion is translucent. Add the pancetta and sorrel leaves to the pan, then stir in the breadcrumbs and season with salt and pepper. »

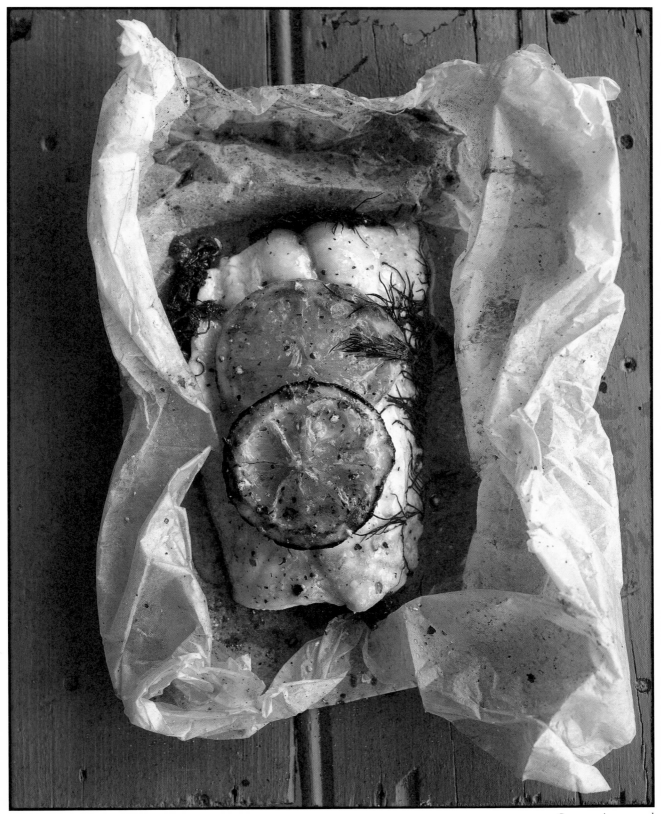

Snapper in a parcel

Put the fish on a baking tray and squeeze lemon juice into the cavity, then season and stuff it with the breadcrumb mixture. Brush both sides of the fish with olive oil, then squeeze over more lemon juice and season. Bake for 15 minutes, then carefully turn the fish over and cook it for another 10–15 minutes. Remove the fish from the oven and allow it to rest for 10 minutes before serving.

FISH STOCK

Makes 1.5 litres

As mentioned, snapper heads make the best fish stock, and if you have fish stock in the freezer you can make a simple soup or a rustic fish stew without a second thought. It also gives you a base for a sauce, or with the addition of the tiniest amount of gelatine (see Glossary) can become a quivering jelly – you could even serve it with poached seafood encased in it.

The addition of ginger to the stock gives an extra dimension to risottos. Just add 1 bruised knob of ginger to the stockpot before simmering. If I'm making a stock for a fish stew I use some fennel if it is in season (if it's not, I add a star anise). If the stock is to be used for a strongly flavoured dish you could use Pernod, and if you don't want to use wine at all you can add verjuice, which has a natural affinity with seafood. Just don't forget to label and date your stock before freezing it, and use it within three months.

1 kg snapper heads	2 tablespoons butter
1 large onion, finely chopped	½ cup (125 ml) dry white wine
1 leek, finely chopped	1.5–2 litres cold water
1 carrot, finely chopped	10 stalks flat-leaf parsley
½ stick celery, finely chopped	1 sprig thyme
¼ small fennel bulb (optional), finely chopped	½ fresh bay leaf

To clean the snapper heads, cut around the pointed underside of the head and the gills, then pull away the whole bottom part of the head and discard. Scrape out any trace of blood or innards, then rinse the head carefully and repeat with the remaining heads.

Put all the vegetables into an enamelled or stainless steel stockpot with the butter and sweat them over low heat for 2 minutes; the vegetables should not brown. Add the fish heads to the stockpot and sweat them for 1 minute more, then increase the heat to high, pour in the wine and boil vigorously for a few minutes. Pour in the cold water, then add the herbs and simmer gently over low heat for 20 minutes, without allowing the stock to boil at any stage – it will become cloudy if allowed to boil.

Strain through a fine sieve or muslin to give a good clear stock. Allow the strained stock to cool and then freeze or refrigerate it if you are not using it within the day. A good fish stock will set into a jelly after refrigeration.

SPRING GREENS

THOUGHTS OF PLANTING MY SPRING GREENS START TO enter my mind as soon as the cold weather hits. There is such a lot of planning to be done to be ready in time. I love winter, yet sometimes feel very lazy – a few stolen hours are more likely to be spent on the couch in front of the fire with a really good book than out in the garden – but this year, for the first time, I started to think about my spring greens in the dead of winter.

This was helped by the fact that I was yet again changing the garden around. Over the years, I've found that unless the vegetables are right in front of my nose every day I risk missing the opportunity to make the most of my harvest. We actually began this change in the soaring heat of January, making five raised garden beds in the spot where visitors used to park their cars too near the entrance to our house. I say 'the entrance' as though it's the front door, yet everyone always enters from the back veranda into the kitchen. In fact I don't know if I even have a key to the front door!

For a variety of reasons absolutely nothing happened with these beds until winter arrived, and that's when preparation really began. Organic loam and mushroom compost by the tonne was needed, as were more old red bricks. It wasn't until the new beds were finished and ready for planting that I suddenly realised the garden was now a little out of scale, because we had had to pull out a large old peach tree that was dying, hedged in against the wall of our huge farm shed, so the backdrop of the garden was suddenly missing. With the roses and shrubs dormant, winter gave me the chance to prune harshly, taking no prisoners, and to reposition many of the shrubs that suddenly seemed too tall in the middle of the garden, given the changes around them. I felt like I had a new landscape to work with and I spent more time than I had to spare poring over plant catalogues and gardening websites – whether for my kitchen garden or orchard, my choice of plants or trees is always guided by flavour. Invariably I seem to choose either a variety that is not readily available, or a plant that needs to be eaten just as it is picked.

I just love having a mixture of roses, vegetables and herbs planted together, but finding seeds for the vegetables I wanted to plant proved difficult, until I came across the website www.theitaliangardener.com.au and www.diggers.com.au, of course. Just finding the seeds for these vegetables was a breakthrough. Then, much more importantly, given my frenetic life and haphazard approach to gardening, I found a very talented person who raised all the seeds to seedlings with such success that I was awash with the plants I had found impossible to buy from nurseries.

Having virgin beds to sow my greens in was such an exciting phase of the garden. I wanted to plant everything all at once so that spring would arrive with a bang, and that's exactly what we did. It's not quite spring as I write this (only August in fact), but the plants, the birds and the orchard are behaving as if spring is already here.

All of my greens have galloped. We've had more frost than normal this year and the

cavolo nero is full of flavour. I probably put the celeriac in too late but it looks so healthy that I'll persevere. I hate to think how many plants of rapini (*cima di rapa* or turnip greens) we put in, but with this early spring weather it's bolting like mad; it grows like a weed and is a little like a cross between a broccoli and a turnip. Picked in big bunches just before dinner each night, it's a green that's become the centre of our evening meals. Simply washed, chopped, blanched and tossed in extra virgin olive oil, it makes fantastic eating – peppery and bitter yet somehow still sweet.

This year I also planted twelve one-year-old asparagus plants, as our older ones had been decimated by rabbits. While I'll have none ready to eat this year, it is so wonderful to see the promise of next year's crop in the form of a spear not much thicker than a matchstick poking through the mounded earth. Behind the asparagus I've planted asparagus peas but I'm still waiting for them to climb.

My chicory is ready to pick, while my garlic, perhaps planted a little late this year, hasn't yet formed to its full potential. Impatient as I am, though, I still picked a few tops and tossed them with a not-quite-formed bulb of Florence fennel while sautéing some baby squid I bought at the Barossa markets on Saturday, and they were delicious. I lost all of my sorrel to the snails, but now that I've learnt that coffee grounds repel them I'm about to ring my herb nursery and place my order.

I have the best position for growing spring lettuces – in a raised bed next to an old porcelain sink for washing the greens. It sits flush against a wall of glass that gets so hot in summer that I've yet to find a crop that survives the intense heat, but winter and spring plantings are protected. I picked my first borage flowers today. I love these delicate blue flowers with black trimmings that taste of cucumber, as they make such a beautiful show – although the plants are so large that I fear they'll crowd out the lettuce.

The big terracotta pots next to the wood-fired oven are lush with sweet marjoram, rosemary, thyme and more flat-leaf parsley. I'm picking great bunches of flat-leaf parsley and my rosemary is awash with pale blue flowers. The beautifully scented lemon thyme bush is abundant with its shiny leaves attached to delicate stems, partly because they are shaded by the borage – no stripping of woody stems is needed here. Then there is orange-peel thyme, so-called for its orange scent and the rough feel of the ground cover, similar to citrus skin. My tarragon plant is just poking its head up from the ground, and to me those first tarragon tips are the very taste of spring.

I got so carried away planting my Italian vegetables that I almost left out my staples, such as spinach and silverbeet. As readily available to buy as they are, my pleasure in the stalks, particularly of the silverbeet, only really comes to the fore when they've been picked fresh from my own garden. At least my local nurseryman has these as seedlings, so as soon as the cavolo nero finishes, there will be space to plant these, and with the warmth of spring, I'll be picking their young leaves within weeks

No two years are the same in our garden – there is just so much to learn and whilst I first wrote this years ago, it's still much the same. The garden is so vital to our lives.

SORREL

My first experience of sorrel was in 1985 in Sydney when I had my first meal at Claude's, then under the direction of that wonderful chef Damien Pignolet, now of Bistro Moncur. It was a Friday night, which meant it was bouillabaisse night: a rich and satisfying meal. Serving sorrel tart before the main course was a brilliant pairing. I went straight home to the Valley and planted this wonderful herb.

Seen growing wild throughout Europe, sorrel also sprouts like a weed in our conditions. It is nonetheless worthwhile having in the garden as it is quite difficult to find at the green-grocer's. Plant in the spring or autumn, water well in summer, and you will have a supply for years: if you cut the plants back at the base when the flower-stalks show, you won't have to replant. (If you aren't assiduous about this, just replant every year or two, unless the original plant has self-seeded.) Sorrel is greatly loved by snails, attracting them like no other herb, but sprinkling coffee grounds in the garden deters them, as it does the millipedes.

While some cookbooks describe sorrel as being similar to spinach, they are really just referring to its growing pattern; it is, rather, a cousin of the equally astringent rhubarb. Sorrel has a particularly piquant, lemony flavour and is a wonderful accompaniment to rich foods such as brains, sweetbreads, eggs, salmon or ocean trout, or oily fish such as herrings and sardines (try wrapping either of these in sorrel leaves and barbecuing them).

Sorrel can become quite strong and rank, so you must be vigilant about tossing over-grown leaves into the compost to ensure that young leaves come through all the time. This way you'll always have baby leaves to add to a salad (they may be a little sharp on their own but they add another dimension to mixed greens).

If you have an overabundance of young leaves, sweat them in a little extra virgin olive oil in a non-reactive frying pan (an aluminium pan will turn black and give the sorrel a metallic taste), until they break down to make their own purée. This mixture can be refrigerated, covered with a film of extra virgin olive oil, in a well-sealed jar for at least ten days. With the addition of onion, the purée can be diluted with chicken or fish stock and cream before being blended in a food processor and served as a simple sauce with any of the foods mentioned on the previous page. If you are not usually keen on cream sauces, bear in mind that the sorrel will cut the richness of the cream.

Sorrel soup can be made in a similar way, too. Cook a large, peeled potato with the sorrel, stock and onion, then put the potato through a potato ricer or food mill (a food processor will turn it into glue) and return it to the soup for reheating with cream stirred through.

Sorrel braised with tomato, lemon and capers is a great base for veal, tuna or chicken. Sweat a diced onion in a little butter and extra virgin olive oil until softened, then add 2 sliced lemons and turn up the heat so that both onion and lemon caramelise just a little. Watch the pan carefully, though, and adjust the temperature if the mixture looks like burning.

Add a handful of trimmed young sorrel leaves. Finely dice several peeled and seeded ripe tomatoes (or preserved or tinned ones, strained of juice) and add them to the sorrel mixture, then season it well and splash in a little more olive oil. The tomato only needs a minute or so over heat to warm through. Stir in a tablespoon each of capers and chopped flat-leaf parsley and let the mixture cool for the flavours to meld while you pan-fry a piece of veal, chicken or tuna. While the meat is resting, quickly reheat the sauce and then serve.

Sorrel Mayonnaise (see page 147) is a good counterpoint to a smoked tongue dish. It can also lift the flavour of a cooked rock lobster that has been refrigerated.

If you ever scramble duck eggs, rich as they are, do so with a good dollop of cream, a knob of butter, salt and freshly ground black pepper. When the eggs are just set, fold through shredded young sorrel leaves and serve.

Looking through old Pheasant Farm Restaurant menus, I now see how often I used to raid my bed of sorrel: smoked potted tongue and sorrel; kid pot-roasted with garlic and sorrel; scrambled guinea-fowl eggs with smoked ocean trout and sorrel; rabbit with a sorrel and mustard sauce; sausage of rabbit fillets, kidneys and livers wrapped in pastry and served with sorrel sauce; lamb with artichokes and sorrel; and fillet of hare with a brandy, peppercorn and sorrel sauce. What an indispensable herb!

OMELETTE WITH SORREL AND ANCHOVY   *Serves 1*

I have an omelette pan that is used for no other purpose: given that no metal implements go near the pan, my omelettes never stick. A pan like this is well worth having. Slow-roasted garlic cloves can also be added to the sorrel filling once it has been piled onto the omelette.

30 g unsalted butter

3 free-range eggs

sea salt flakes and freshly ground
    black pepper

2 tablespoons cream

2 tablespoons verjuice

good handful young sorrel leaves, trimmed

1 anchovy fillet, finely chopped

squeeze of lemon juice (optional)

Melt half the butter in an omelette pan and allow it to cool a little. Break the eggs into a bowl, then add the melted butter with a pinch of salt and a grind of pepper and beat lightly with a fork. Set aside.

Reduce the cream and verjuice by half in a small enamelled or stainless steel saucepan, then add the sorrel and anchovy. Check the seasoning, adding a squeeze of lemon juice if required. The sorrel will form its own purée in just a few minutes. Keep warm.

Melt the remaining butter in the omelette pan over medium heat, coating the base with the butter as it melts. When the butter is nut-brown, pour in the eggs, stirring quickly with a heat-resistant plastic spatula or wooden spoon. Lift the edge gently as it cooks to allow more uncooked egg to run underneath. The omelette must be shiny and very moist in the centre. When it is almost cooked, spoon the warm sorrel mixture into the centre, then turn the omelette onto itself as you slide it onto a warmed plate. Rub an extra bit of butter over the top – it melts in wonderfully. Serve immediately.

SORREL TART   *Serves 6–8*

Sorrel tart is one of my tried and true favourites. This is the tart I made from memory, helped by a recipe of Richard Olney's in his *Simple French Food*, after eating Damien Pignolet's memorable sorrel tart. I like to serve it as a first course, sometimes with crème fraîche (matching piquant with piquant). It also partners smoked salmon or gravlax well.

1 × quantity Sour-cream Pastry
    (see page 151)

600 g young sorrel leaves

2 onions, finely chopped

butter, for cooking

6 large free-range eggs

650 ml cream

sea salt flakes and freshly ground
    black pepper

Make and chill the pastry as instructed, then roll out and use to line a 20 cm springform tin. Chill the pastry case for 20 minutes. »

Preheat the oven to 200°C. Line the pastry case with foil, then cover with pastry weights. Blind bake the pastry case for 15 minutes, then remove the foil and weights and bake for a further 5 minutes. Remove from the oven and reset the temperature to 190°C.

Strip the sorrel leaves from their stems, then wash the leaves carefully and drain well. Sweat the onions slowly in an enamelled or stainless steel saucepan over low heat with a knob of butter until softened, being careful not to let them colour. Add the sorrel leaves and cook with the onion for just a few minutes until a purée forms. Remove the pan from the heat and allow to cool a little. If you prefer a very fine purée, blend the onion and sorrel in a food processor.

Beat the eggs and add the cream, salt and pepper. Stir the sorrel purée into the egg mixture. Pour the filling into the still-warm pastry case and bake until set, 40–50 minutes for a deep tin (a shallower tin may only need 15–20 minutes). The tart will continue to set a little once it has been removed from the oven. Serve warm or at room temperature. Leftovers cold from the fridge are pretty good, too.

SPINACH AND SILVERBEET

As a child I always wondered about Popeye's love of spinach, my least favourite vegetable back then. In fact, I only knew of silverbeet, rather than true spinach, cooked to blazes, stalks and all, in an aluminium saucepan. The stalks were grey and lifeless and the leaves soggy and unappetising.

Thankfully, things have changed. Now I'm happy to eat spinach or silverbeet cooked to perfection – that is, quickly, so that the stalks still have a slight crunch and are almost sweet. I would quite happily eat a plate of silverbeet stalks on their own, drizzled with extra virgin olive oil and seasoned with sea salt and freshly ground black pepper, thank you very much. When I think back on the lost opportunities of my youth . . .

It did remind me, though, of how easily a vegetable can become overlooked, when I think of how I reacted to the availability of English spinach for the first time. I pushed silverbeet to the side completely until the time I ate it straight from a friend's garden, when I literally fought with my host for the stalks – English spinach stalks are not nearly so special.

Spinach and silverbeet have so many uses and are easy to grow in most areas, looking vibrantly healthy in the vegie garden for very little effort. They can even be beautiful. The lighter-coloured leaves of Swiss chard, milder in flavour than silverbeet, sit atop stalks of pink, red and the most vivid yellow (like my meyer lemons, I decided).

Another form of silverbeet, called perpetual spinach beet, is also worth considering planting; you simply pick the small leaves as you want them over months and the plant continues to grow.

Back to traditional English spinach. The young leaves are great raw in a salad, while mature leaves are better cooked. Wash the leaves well (no snails, please, or, for South Australians, millipedes), then chop them.

Cook the leaves in just the water that clings to them after you wash them, until they collapse. While I love to anoint my spinach with extra virgin olive oil, butter melted over the hot leaves is just as good – and, as spinach is so good for us, this addition is fine in my book.

If you have reluctant greens-eaters in your family, try starting them on raw young leaves prepared in any of the ways suggested below. Once they are hooked, then pounce with beautifully cooked and seasoned spinach. Well, that's the way I thought it would work with my first two grandchildren, Zöe and Max. They used to love almost any food, from

raw fish to anchovies, sweet cloves of caramelised garlic to mushrooms and offal – yet greens were 'enemy number one'.

Always keen to take on a challenge, my first offering was cooked spinach topped by a perfectly poached egg, all on a great slab of toast. The second was a salad of raw leaves with chopped freshly boiled egg, toasted pine nuts and currants soaked in a little verjuice to plump them up. No luck.

Rotolo, where a large sheet of pasta is used to roll up a filling of spinach, caramelised garlic, oregano and ricotta flavoured with just a hint of nutmeg, is an institution in my family (see below), so it seemed a sure winner. Zöe and Max helped make the pasta first, in a major morning's work, but it still didn't win them over. At least the grown-ups enjoyed the end result.

My quest continued. Spinach pasta never actually works for me – I find it tends to lack flavour – although spinach gnocchi does (as long as every last bit of water is wrung out of the cooked spinach), but not for Zöe and Max. My final attempt was a combination of some of the earlier efforts: a salad of young spinach leaves topped with caramelised garlic and a perfectly poached egg (with toast soldiers to dip into it), and anchovy mayonnaise on the side (see page 109). When a request was made for more soldiers I thought success was at hand, but they were used to mop up the last of the anchovy mayonnaise – the spinach languished on the plate.

Oh, well. With luck, as they all grow up, my grandchildren's tastes will change, just as mine did. In the meantime, I'll continue to eat spinach whenever I can.

ROTOLO DI SPINACI   *Serves 8–10*

This recipe is based on one in *The River Café Cookbook*, by Rose Gray and Ruth Rogers, and it also appeared in *Stephanie Alexander and Maggie Beer's Tuscan Cookbook*. It is a dish I have cooked so many times, both with students and when Stephanie and I were on tour launching the book, that making it has become second nature.

verjuice, for soaking

40 g dried porcini

1 tablespoon butter

1 red onion, finely chopped

1 tablespoon oregano leaves, chopped

800 g spinach, washed, blanched
  and chopped

finely chopped rind of 1 lemon

3 tablespoons extra virgin olive oil

2 cloves garlic, chopped

250 g field mushrooms *or* fresh porcini,
  roughly sliced

sea salt flakes and freshly ground
  black pepper

350 g ricotta

80 g freshly grated Parmigiano Reggiano,
  plus extra to serve

freshly grated nutmeg, to taste

PASTA DOUGH

3⅓ cups (500 g) unbleached strong flour
  (see Glossary)

½ teaspoon sea salt

1 large (55 g) free-range egg

6 large free-range egg yolks

semolina flour, for dusting

For the pasta dough, put the flour and salt into a food processor and add the egg and egg yolks. Pulse until the pasta begins to come together into a loose ball of dough. Knead the pasta dough on a workbench dusted with semolina flour for about 3 minutes or until it is smooth.

Divide the dough into quarters and roll each piece into a ball. Wrap the pieces of dough in plastic film and refrigerate for at least 20 minutes or up to 2 hours.

Meanwhile, for the filling, warm some verjuice in a saucepan, then use to reconstitute the dried porcini – this will take about 15–20 minutes.

Heat the butter in a frying pan and cook the onion until softened, then add the oregano, spinach and lemon rind. Stir to combine, then let cool.

Drain the porcini, reserving the strained soaking liquid. Wash the porcini to remove any grit. Heat the olive oil in a frying pan and gently cook the garlic for a few minutes over low heat. Add the field mushrooms or fresh porcini and cook, stirring, over high heat for 5 minutes. Add the soaked porcini and cook gently over low heat for 20 minutes, adding a little of the strained soaking liquid at a time to keep the mushrooms moist. Add the rest of the soaking liquid – you may need to turn up the heat to evaporate the remaining juices. Season and let cool. When cold, roughly chop.

Put the ricotta in a large bowl and break it up lightly with a fork, then add the spinach mixture, the Parmigiano Reggiano and a generous amount of nutmeg. Add salt and pepper, if necessary, and set aside.

Using a pasta machine, put a piece of pasta dough through the maximum setting, then repeat another 8–10 times until shiny and silky, each time folding one end into the centre and the other over this, then giving the dough a turn to the right before rolling it again. Once this has been done, put the dough through the other settings (going through 8–10 times on each setting) until you reach the second-last setting, then put it through twice. You should have a 30 × 10 cm pasta sheet. Repeat this process with the remaining 3 pieces

of dough. Join 2 sheets of pasta together at their longest edge, brushing the edges with water to seal, to make a sheet about 30 × 20 cm. Repeat with the remaining 2 sheets of pasta, then trim the edges to straighten them.

Working in two batches, transfer each joined sheet of pasta to a large, clean tea towel – choose one that is as smooth as possible as any texture will leave a pattern – and position it so the longer edge faces you. Spoon half the mushroom mixture in a 3 cm-wide line along the long edge of the pasta nearest you. Cover the rest of the pasta with half the spinach and ricotta mixture. Starting with the edge nearest you, gently roll up the pasta into a log 6 cm in diameter and 30 cm long, working away from you and using the tea towel to help guide you. Wrap the rotolo in the tea towel as tightly as possible, folding the edges in to secure the parcel, then tie it with kitchen string to hold it in shape during cooking. Repeat with the remaining pasta sheet and fillings.

Bring a fish kettle or large deep roasting pan of salted water to the boil. Carefully slip in a wrapped rotolo, making sure it is submerged, then cover and simmer over low heat for 18–20 minutes. Carefully remove the rotolo, turn it upside-down, and keep it warm while cooking the second.

Transfer the rotoli to a chopping board, carefully unwrap and cut into 3 cm-thick slices. Serve 2 slices per person and offer extra grated Parmigiano Reggiano at the table.

SALAD OF SPINACH WITH POACHED EGG AND ANCHOVY MAYONNAISE

Serves 4

When making the mayonnaise, simply mash in anchovies to taste as you blend the egg yolks before adding the oil.

1 × quantity Anchovy Mayonnaise (see page 147)	4 slices crusty bread
2 bunches baby spinach leaves	1 tablespoon verjuice *or* vinegar
8 cloves garlic, peeled	4 free-range eggs (use the freshest eggs
⅓ cup (80 ml) extra virgin olive oil	possible for a perfect result)

Make the mayonnaise following the instructions and set aside.

Preheat the oven to 200°C. Pick through the spinach, rejecting any bruised or old leaves. Wash the leaves very well, then spin or pat dry. Blanch the garlic in a saucepan of boiling water for 4 minutes, then drain and infuse in the olive oil in a small frying pan over low heat until golden. Remove the garlic from the oil and set both aside.

Brush the bread with the garlicky oil and toast in the oven until golden, then cut into strips to make 'soldiers' for dipping.

Warm the plates, but only to just above room temperature, so that the mayonnaise doesn't melt. »

Two-thirds fill a deep stainless steel frying pan with water, then add a spoonful of verjuice or vinegar and bring the pan to a rolling boil over high heat. Crack the eggs onto a plate (or into 4 coffee cups), then slide them into the water as quickly as possible and turn the heat down to a simmer. Cook for 3 minutes, so that the white has just set but the yolk is runny. (If you don't have a helper in the kitchen, you can slip the eggs into a bowl of cold water to stop them cooking, although it's better to serve them immediately. Just remember to drain them on kitchen paper just before serving.)

Warm the garlic gently in the reserved oil, then toss the spinach through, just to warm it. Divide the spinach and garlic cloves between the plates, then add a poached egg and a good dollop of the mayonnaise and position the soldiers.

WATERCRESS

No one has ever offered me a watercress sandwich at an afternoon tea party. Perhaps it's because I never attend such events, or are they, like the sandwiches themselves, a thing of the past? There are, however, plenty of literary references to thinly sliced, white buttered-bread sandwiches with a watercress filling – somehow these are always 'dainty'. Only butter is used (never margarine), there is not a tea bag in sight, and fine china cups are de rigueur in the drawing rooms where these sandwiches are served.

While not a participant in afternoon tea parties, I have always loved watercress. In fact, I used to collect it in the spring from a nearby creek where it grew in such profusion that we'd pick buckets and buckets of it. Then one of my staff declared her concern that the grazing animals upstream might be polluting the water and that liver fluke could be present. As I'd been using the watercress for years, I was a little cavalier about the matter. But in the past two years we haven't had enough rain for the creek to run, so I've had to find another source anyway.

If you find watercress in the wild and are not sure of the water source, it is best to wash it thoroughly before cooking. Better still, if you have a pond in your garden you can transplant wild rooted watercress, but don't try planting it in your vegie garden – it just won't work, particularly with water restrictions.

Although I can imagine the sense of satisfaction at having such easy access to this delicious plant – and, as they say, it grows like a weed given the right environment – it is readily available from commercial herb growers.

Be selective, though, when choosing a bunch of watercress as it wilts quickly. Look for fresh, bright-looking leaves and stems, and refrigerate it after washing, either wrapped in kitchen paper inside a wet tea towel or in a jug of water covered with a plastic bag (remember to change the water daily).

Once you become addicted to the peppery hit watercress provides, you'll wonder how you ever lived without it. Watercress is a great foil to either very rich or quite bland flavours: try it with eggs, goat's cheese or ricotta. Add it to any other salad leaves, except rocket or nasturtium, which are peppery enough on their own. From bitter witlof to crispy iceberg, watercress provides a great contrast.

Toss watercress through a warm salad of waxy potatoes and hard-boiled eggs. Serve it with wedges of orange and sliced fennel with a dressing of good olive oil, orange juice and red-wine vinegar. Season with sea salt, but don't bother with pepper.

To make watercress mayonnaise, thoroughly wash a bunch of watercress, then strip away the leaves and dry them well. Mash the leaves to a paste with a little garlic and a good squeeze of lemon juice, then add to a homemade mayonnaise (make sure the emulsion is quite thick). Serve with grilled fish or poached chicken.

WATERCRESS AND BROAD BEAN SOUP   *Serves 6*

Watercress soups are just about as well-documented as the infamous sandwiches. I've always found them too peppery for my liking and therefore have succumbed in the past to adding a lot of cream. So, faced with a huge bunch of watercress that was too limp to use in a salad after a very hot drive home from the market, I decided to make my own version of watercress soup. I rejected the very tired stems, then collected broad beans from the garden to add a touch of sweetness. The balance was perfect and I didn't need to add any cream – and the soup is just as good cold as hot, which makes it perfect for a warm spring day.

If you prefer, you can substitute peas for the broad beans. You'll find frozen peas useful to have on hand as sadly they're often in much better condition than the 'fresh' peas you buy to shell yourself, unless you're lucky.

60 g butter
1 tablespoon olive oil
1 large onion, diced
500 g shelled broad beans
    (about 1 kg unshelled)
1 large bunch watercress
    (to yield 3 cups chopped leaves
    after washing and trimming)

sea salt flakes
1 litre Golden Chicken Stock
    (see page 149)
plain yoghurt and freshly picked chervil,
    to serve

Melt the butter with the oil in a heavy-based stainless steel, enamelled or non-stick saucepan. Add the onion and cook for a few minutes, then stir in the broad beans, coating them with butter. Sauté gently over low heat for 5 minutes. Stir in the chopped watercress, then add the salt and stock. Simmer until the broad beans are tender (the exact time will depend on their age), but don't over-cook or you'll lose the brilliant green colour. Purée the mixture, then adjust the seasoning. Serve hot or cold with a dollop of yoghurt and a little fresh chervil.

SPRING LAMB

ONE OF THE MOST OBVIOUS SPRING DELIGHTS IS LAMB.
Spring lamb is the meat from lambs born in autumn and sold the following spring, so is usually from animals between four and six months old. The tender, juicy sweetness of the meat is a direct result of the nutritious diet the animals enjoy during their short lives. They are firstly suckled on mother's milk for a period (usually six to eight weeks, but sometimes longer), and then moved on to graze the verdant grasses of late winter/early spring.

I much prefer to eat breeds grown for their meat rather than their wool, and happily my two favourite breeds are both readily available to me. One is the 'pure Suffolk', a breed in which both sides of the gene pool come from meat stock. This would have to be described as the *crème de la crème* of lamb, and is grown south of Adelaide by Richard Gunner of Coorong Angus Beef. The other is a White Suffolk/Merino cross, cuts of which are available every Saturday at my local Barossa Farmers' Market, from John and Jan Angas of Hutton Vale.

It has taken a long time to have lamb for sale branded by breed and it is a practice that needs encouragement, since there is such a difference in the texture and flavour of the breeds mentioned above compared to the Merino, which is bred primarily for wool. As well as spring lamb from Suffolk and other meat breeds, another flavour treat is milk-fed lamb. It is a real delicacy – the meat is sweet, tender and buttery with such a special texture as well as a clean flavour. It lends itself wonderfully to slow-braising in extra virgin olive oil and verjuice with rosemary, or quick grilling on a barbecue then resting in a marinade. The meat also works beautifully with the Mediterranean tradition of spit-roasting whole, or being separated into shoulder and leg joints for slow-cooking and grilling, respectively. For centuries, Italians have headed for the hills at Easter to feast on platters of grilled milk-fed lamb (*abbacchio*). Two legs (each about 1 kg) will feed six, with an anchovy or garlic mayonnaise and a peppery salad to go with them.

While Australian producers may not have an ancient culinary tradition of their own to fall back on, they learn continually from countries with more entrenched food cultures that share a climate similar to ours. For example, in recent times we have enjoyed the marvellous milk-fed lamb of several producers Australia-wide, the first of which was from Illabo.

In 1994, Tony Lehmann of Illabo, in southern New South Wales, saw a niche and began to sell his milk-fed lambs to top-class restaurants and a few specialist retailers in Sydney, including Leichhardt's AC Butchery. His Border Leicester Merino Poll Dorset cross provides lambs varying in size from 8–12 kg, raised purely on their mother's milk for approximately eight weeks. Tony has been incredibly successful in his operation.

Once a niche market is established, other producers are tempted to join in. And now it's time for me to declare my hand. Years ago as an adjunct to her Barossa Farm Produce business, my elder daughter, Saskia, set up a project to produce milk-fed lamb with the assistance of a very motivated and innovative group of farmers. She gave them her require-ments for the product she wanted to cook, and together they worked on a cross-breeding program to ensure flavour and texture. Saskia believed the differences in breeds, as well as the Barossa climate and pasture, would give their lamb a distinctive flavour.

Each chef who used this lamb completed a 'trace-back' sheet so the farmer received direct feedback. Collectively, these have formed a quality manual, useful not only at the farm gate but at the processors, where costs are high (only a niche market can support the cost of processing such a small animal) and where careful, humane han-dling is essential for the best results.

This is paddock-to-plate planning, and the outcome was stunning. The lamb is like the Italian *abbacchio*, which is so buttery and succulent; I was amazed by its delicate yet full-flavoured texture and the generous amount of meat. Its sweetness goes so well with all those Mediterranean flavours: olive oil, rosemary, golden shallots, preserved lemons, bay leaves, dill, garlic – and even my favourite, slow-roasted quinces. But all this is history now.

Much of this milk-fed lamb was exported to Japan or sold direct to restaurants. Some of this used to find its way to my kitchen for special occasions – often it's the shoulder (to my mind the sweetest cut of all) as her restaurant customers invariably want the legs or the saddle. However, this venture was the beginning of her entrepreneurial drive, which has led her to always value the conversation between the farmer and the cook.

Most butchers are incredibly friendly, and certainly those of the old school know a great deal about their trade and are only too happy to help with advice. So many people buy on price only, not understanding the differences in quality. In these times of course it is important to receive value for money – yet you should still try to make an informed choice about the meat you are buying. I always want to know about the animal's life and if it has been respected in death, as this has so much to do with quality and sustainability.

I don't see as much evidence of it these days, but larger retailers used to package whole sides of lamb showcasing the leg at the top and advertise it for a ridiculously low price. To the person in a hurry it seemed to be a good buy, as a leg of lamb these days is many times the price of the rest of the carcass, but the use of 'lamb' as a descriptor was stretching it, and you got what you paid for – low-grade meat.

If it is still done then I guess it is clever marketing because under the leg would be the lesser cuts of meat, which are more likely to be wasted. These lesser cuts, if cooked correctly, can make good honest meals – say by pot-roasting the shoulder (though this would be better if sold in one piece and not as chops), or by making a stew or curry. My main complaint is the insistence of so many people who buy just on price to use these neck, shoulder or chump chops of inferior meat as barbecue chops. They are served up as leathery offerings and considered a proper meal. There is no food I dislike more, and it could fast make me a vegetarian!

In Australia, lamb is not classified by age, but instead on the eruption of teeth, so the moment the first baby tooth falls out is when lamb becomes hogget (usually at about twelve months old). Mutton is the meat from sheep over two years old. Many farmers prefer the taste of mutton to lamb and hogget, as it has a depth of flavour missing from the younger meat. I have to say my husband shows his Mallala upbringing in loving a rolled, seasoned mutton flap. His family never bothered with spring lamb, probably because it was that much more expensive than mutton or hogget.

If you get the chance to try saltbush mutton you'll be in for a treat. It has a superb flavour from the saltbush the lamb feeds on. Saltbush mutton can be bought from butchers in Quorn and further north in South Australia. It should definitely be slow-roasted – the ultimate 'baked dinner' in my opinion (see page 123). Try cooking it using the same method as that for a leg of kid (see page 68), pot-roasting very slowly with garlic and rosemary and adding just half a cup of stock at a time so that the juices become thick and caramelised.

So what should you look for in spring lamb? To start with, it should be stamped with a red vegetable-dye brand that validates it as coming from a young animal – the younger the animal, the pinker and more finely grained the meat (the lamb now available in spring is from animals about four months old).

While the quality of spring lamb is generally good, it's not always consistent, and this can be for several reasons. Regardless of the age of the animal, stress produces darker, tougher meat, so the issue of how the animal is handled becomes a factor. This concern has been recognised by Meat and Livestock Australia and the sheep industry, with both determined to improve handling to give consistency to the Australian market first and then break into export markets.

Remember, let your butcher guide you. Ask about the differences in price, suggested cooking methods and final taste. A prime cut of spring lamb will be at least twice the price

of an inferior cut, but will taste ten times better. If cost is a limiting factor, then just serve a smaller, perfectly cooked portion as the highlight of the meal instead of the filler.

With improved farm management we have many more options than just spring lamb these days. However, there are questions you really must ask your butcher. Is it lamb, in fact, or mutton, or even hogget? All can be terrific, but the dishes you use them in and the cooking times required will differ significantly.

For lunch at the restaurant we used to make shoulder of baby lamb and pickled quince pies, and when we ran out of lamb, we used mutton – the cooking had to be varied markedly and the flavour was totally different, but the pies still made great eating. However, as soon as we offered a mutton and pickled quince pie on the menu, sales dropped off so dramatically we decided it wasn't worth it. Perhaps this made me understand a little more why truth in labelling is something butchers might feel is too hard to handle.

Cooking a leg of lamb on the bone gives maximum flavour and all the meat needs is a couple of bay leaves and a few sprigs of rosemary tucked into it. Always take the meat out of the refrigerator 2 hours before cooking to allow it to come to room temperature. Smear the skin with olive oil, stick slivers of garlic and bay leaves or sprigs of rosemary into little pockets cut with a sharp knife, then season with sea salt and freshly ground black pepper and roast.

If carving at the table puts you off cooking a roast leg of lamb, you can ask your butcher to butterfly the leg – that is, flatten it out so it's an even thickness and you can barbecue it in one piece – or have the butcher remove the thigh bone while retaining the shank, which keeps the joint intact. Called an easy-carve lamb leg, this really does make carving so much easier. Or you could ask for the leg to be tunnel-boned. You can then fill the cavity with a paste made from garlic and rosemary. Or you could use mushrooms chopped and sautéed with spring onion, or make an anchovy butter, adding some garlic and lemon juice. Let it sit for at least 30 minutes for the flavours to penetrate (or it can be left overnight in the refrigerator). A couple of lengths of cooking twine will keep the stuffing in place and maintain the shape of the joint. While this cut is a good idea, it does cook a little quicker than a normal leg of lamb – and remember that meat cooked on the bone always has the best flavour of all.

If you wish to bone and butterfly a leg of lamb yourself, turn a slightly larger leg on to its less fatty side. Using a sharp knife, cut right down the bone from the wide to the thin end of the leg. Carefully cut the bone out, slipping your knife under it and cutting it away from the sinew. Remove the bone, then open out the meat and pound it until it is about

2.5 cm thick all over, then stuff as described earlier, or marinate. For pink lamb, cook on the barbecue or under an efficient griller about 15 cm from the heat source for 15 minutes a side. If barbecuing, baste it with the marinade, if using, every 10 minutes. Throw some eggplant slices on the grill, then serve the lot with pesto.

For roasting, as a guide preheat the oven to 180°C, place the boned lamb leg in a roasting pan, then drizzle with olive oil and season to taste. Roast it for 15 minutes per 500 g, then rest it in a warm place for 20–30 minutes before carving.

It takes five minutes to prepare a leg of lamb; if the joint is around 2 kg it will take 60–80 minutes at around 200°C to cook, but it need only be attended to once – and that's only when you add the potatoes to the baking dish. What could be simpler? Well, possibly eschewing the usual roasted vegies and instead layering potato, onion and garlic (or perhaps eggplant, tomato and onion) in a baking dish and setting the leg of lamb straight on the rack above. Don't want to use the oven? Roast the lamb in a hooded barbecue: it will only take about an hour and you can sit it in a pan atop the potato or eggplant combinations above, if you want a great accompaniment – and no washing up!

But perhaps the easiest cut of all for roasting – or pan-frying or barbecuing – is a rack of lamb. A few tips are well worth noting, however, as not every butcher prepares a rack the same way. Ask the butcher to saw through the chine bone without removing it; the yellow membrane should be discarded. A properly trimmed rack should be free of any shoulder bone remnants. To do this, the butcher cuts off the fat and meat from the edge of the fillet to expose the bones, removing the outer membrane. Some might also trim excess fat, but remember that fat is flavour! The butcher then scrapes the exposed bones clean with a sharp knife, so each rib shows separately. You can rub a rack of lamb with garlic and rosemary paste before cooking or perhaps brush it with a quince or plum glaze. And the beauty of a rack is that it needs only about 20 minutes at 200°C with 15 minutes' resting time. If barbecuing a rack, turn the meat frequently so it doesn't burn but caramelises instead.

While I now like to cook lamb racks with a quince glaze (see page 120), one of the classic dishes of provincial France is rack of lamb roasted with a mustard glaze. It combines beautifully with a sorrel sauce and boiled waxy potatoes, or roasted garlic and a salad of bitter greens. This marinade is inspired by one in *Mastering the Art of French Cooking, Volume One*, by Simone Beck, Louisette Bertholle and Julia Child. Blend mustard, soy sauce, a small clove of crushed garlic, some rosemary or thyme, and a pinch of ground ginger in a bowl. Gradually whisk in olive oil, drop by drop, to make a mayonnaise-like cream. Paint the lamb with the mixture – the meat will pick up more flavour if it is coated several hours before roasting.

For those in a hurry, spring lamb will cook very quickly and needs little preparation. The butcher can cut a leg of lamb into steaks for grilling or barbecuing. They can also section the leg into the silverside, topside and flank to make small roasts.

The under-fillet or tenderloin (the smaller part of a loin chop) provides the quickest fix of all: brush the meat with olive oil and sprinkle with oregano dried on the stalk, then pan-fry gently in the oil and squeeze on lemon juice to deglaze the pan. The meat will be ready before you have had time to cook the vegetables.

Lamb loin chops will grill in just 10 minutes. Don't be worried about the fat on the loin chops or saddle. Cook these cuts with the fat on – the flavour of the lamb is so much better this way – then by all means cut it off before eating if it worries you. You can barbecue double-cut loin chops until the outside is crisp and brown and the inside pink and moist. On such a chop, the normally rejected fat sizzles irresistibly on the barbecue and is almost my favourite morsel of the meat. You will need to visit a butcher for these chops rather than buying them pre-cut on a polystyrene tray.

And don't forget the beautifully sweet meat of the shoulder, which can be boned and stuffed with olives, walnuts and lemon rind or cut into cubes for a stir-fry or curry. This will need less cooking than the cheaper cuts that need long, slow cooking in a crockpot. If young it suits spit-roasting as the fat keeps the meat moist during cooking. I use the neck, another sweet cut, for slow-cooking, putting it in the oven in the morning at the lowest of temperatures – add preserved lemons or Pickled Quinces (see page 150). I have to add that the shoulder is, without a doubt, my favourite cut of lamb.

Just remember to cook spring lamb quickly at a high temperature and then let it rest, or seal and then cook at a very low temperature. Lamb should be served pink (and by that I don't mean raw); resist the temptation to overcook it as you will miss out on the taste sensations I have been talking about. Again, ask your butcher for cooking tips.

ROAST LEG OF SUFFOLK LAMB   *Serves 6*

1 × 3 kg leg lamb

3 sprigs rosemary, leaves picked
  and finely chopped

¼ cup (60 ml) extra virgin olive oil

3 cloves garlic, sliced lengthways into 4

2 tablespoons sea salt flakes

½ cup (125 ml) verjuice

Remove the lamb from the refrigerator 2 hours before cooking to allow it to come to room temperature. Preheat the oven to 180°C. Combine the rosemary and olive oil and then rub all over the lamb skin. Make 12 incisions in the skin evenly over the surface of the lamb and insert garlic slices. Rub liberally with salt.

Place the lamb in a roasting pan and roast for 30 minutes. Turn the oven down to 160°C. Turn the lamb leg over and cook for another 20 minutes. Turn the lamb leg over again and cook for another 30 minutes. Turn the oven off and leave the lamb in the oven for 30 minutes with the door ajar.

Remove from the oven, pour off the pan juices into a tall jug and refrigerate the juices to solidify the fat so it can be skimmed from the surface. Leave the lamb to rest in a warm place for another 30 minutes. Remove the fat from the juices, then place the pan juices and verjuice in a saucepan and reduce over high heat to serve as a jus.

Serve with a green olive tapenade and labna.

Roast leg of Suffolk lamb

LAMB SHOULDER POT-ROASTED WITH GARLIC

Serves 4

1.5 kg shoulder lamb

¼–⅓ cup (60–80 ml) extra virgin olive oil

3 sprigs rosemary

sea salt flakes and freshly ground
    black pepper

1 cup (250 ml) verjuice *or* white wine

4 heads garlic, separated into cloves
    but unpeeled

2 cups (500 ml) Golden Chicken Stock
    (see page 149)

chopped flat-leaf parsley, to serve

In a large heavy-based saucepan over low heat, brown the shoulder gently in the olive oil with the rosemary, and season. Pour off any excess oil and deglaze the pan with the verjuice or white wine with the heat turned up high. Add the garlic cloves and stock and bring to the boil. Cook, covered, on a very low heat for about 2 hours or until the meat is tender, turning occasionally. Be careful that the liquid doesn't evaporate, leaving the meat stuck to the bottom of the pan.

Remove the garlic cloves and cool before squeezing them out of their skins to serve alongside the lamb. Take the meat out of the pan and allow to rest, covered in foil, while you make the sauce. Skim the fat from the surface of the cooking liquid and heat, reducing a little. Garnish with chopped flat-leaf parsley and serve with mashed potatoes.

RACK OF LAMB WITH QUINCE GLAZE

Serves 2

2 × 4-rib racks of lamb

2 cloves garlic

½ teaspoon salt

3 sprigs rosemary, leaves picked

1 teaspoon quince paste

¼ cup (60 ml) verjuice

extra virgin olive oil, for cooking

Preheat the oven to 220°C. Ask the butcher to French-trim your racks of lamb, then wrap the exposed bones in foil to stop them burning. Using the flat side of a large knife, crush the garlic with a little salt to make a paste, then transfer it to a bowl. Add the rosemary, quince paste, 1 tablespoon of the verjuice and a little olive oil and stir to combine into a paste.

Massage the paste all over the lamb. Place the racks upright in a roasting pan and roast for 12–15 minutes for lamb still pink in the centre, or until cooked to desired doneness. If the verjuice and olive oil coat the entire surface of the meat, it should be sealed and caramelised in this time, but test by pushing a skewer into the fattest part of the meat. The skewer should feel warm to the touch and pink juices should be evident; if the skewer is still cool, then the meat is not cooked.

Remove lamb racks from the oven, turn them on their sides, then add another 2 tablespoons verjuice and a little more olive oil to the pan. Rest the lamb for 10 minutes before serving with garlicky mashed potatoes and pan juices.

PETER WALL'S LAMB, BARLEY AND CINNAMON CASSEROLE *Serves 4*

My friend Peter Wall has a special place in my life. He is the one who believed in my quest to make verjuice, and indeed made it possible. Peter loves to cook – I suspect as respite from a very cerebral life. Some thirty years ago it was Peter who taught me to make butter puff pastry and fondant, two things I'm sad to say I don't have the time to make these days. But our shared family meals continue, and it has become something of a tradition for Peter to cook for us that most welcome first meal after I return from business trips or holidays, as everyone knows that travel leaves you both tired and yearning for a home-cooked meal.

Peter served this absolutely melt-in-the-mouth dish of lamb and barley for one such meal after an exhausting trip to Dubai recently. We loved it so much that I cooked it for *The Cook and The Chef* program on the ABC.

This is a marriage of comfort food with fabulous flavour, and it is even better the second day, if you are strong-willed enough not to eat it all in one sitting.

extra virgin olive oil, for cooking

1 kg shoulder lamb, boned and cut into
   2.5 cm cubes (reserve the bones)

400 g pork belly, boned and cut into
   2 cm pieces

1 red onion, chopped

2 cloves garlic, crushed

100 ml red wine

2 tablespoons red-wine vinegar

1 × 410 g can tomatoes, chopped and
   juice reserved

2 cups (500 ml) Golden Chicken Stock
   (see page 149)

1 teaspoon black peppercorns

3 cm cinnamon stick

3–4 sprigs thyme

1 sprig rosemary

350 g pearl barley

salt

Preheat the oven to 125°C. Heat a little oil in a large frying pan over high heat, then add the lamb and seal on all sides. Transfer to a large flameproof casserole dish with a lid, along with the lamb bones. Add the pork to the frying pan and brown, then transfer to the casserole dish. Add a little more oil to the frying pan, then cook the onion and garlic over medium–high heat until browned and add to the meat.

Place the casserole over high heat, then deglaze the pan with the red wine and vinegar. Add the tomatoes and their juice, the chicken stock, spices and herbs. Place the covered casserole in the oven and cook for 3 hours, adjusting the heat if necessary to keep it simmering.

Meanwhile, cook the barley in a large saucepan of boiling salted water for 30–45 minutes or until tender, then drain. After the casserole has been in the oven for 3 hours, add the cooked barley, stir to combine, then cook for another hour. The barley will become almost like a risotto, taking up most of the juices in the dish.

Remove the cinnamon stick and serve.

BARBECUED LAMB CUTLETS   *Serves 4*

4 heads garlic	1 clove garlic, thinly sliced
extra virgin olive oil, for cooking	1 teaspoon finely chopped rosemary
4 double-cut lamb cutlets	sea salt flakes and freshly ground
(2 bones in each cutlet)	black pepper

Wrap the whole heads of garlic in foil, then cut in half widthways and brush the cut sides with olive oil. These will take about 20 minutes to cook on the barbecue, so you'll need to start them before the lamb.

Spike the lamb cutlets with slivers of garlic. Combine the rosemary with the barest trace of olive oil (so as not to flare the barbecue) then rub this mixture over the surface of the meat. Season with salt and pepper.

Place the cutlets on the barbecue, fat-edge down and seal well, then seal each side of the cutlet, turning often enough so the meat does not char. It will take about 12 minutes of cooking altogether. Rest the meat for 5–10 minutes before serving. Drizzle plenty of oil over the garlic head halves and serve alongside the meat.

ROAST SALTBUSH MUTTON

Serves 8–10

The fat content of mutton keeps the meat moist but makes it more susceptible to burning. It is important to watch that the juices do not burn in the bottom of the pan, as they will become bitter and taint the overall flavour. If this happens, you will need to change or clean the pan and return the meat to the oven for the balance of the cooking time.

1 cup (250 ml) port	4 sprigs rosemary, leaves stripped
1 × 3.5 kg leg saltbush mutton	sea salt flakes and freshly ground
extra virgin olive oil, for cooking	black pepper
4 cloves garlic, thickly sliced	

Preheat the oven to 180°C. Gently warm half the port in a small stainless steel saucepan over medium heat. Rinse the lamb under cold water, then dry it well and put it in a lightly oiled roasting pan. Cut tiny pockets into the meat, then poke garlic slices into them. Pour the warm port over the leg, scatter with the rosemary leaves, then season with salt and pepper.

Roast the leg for 2 hours, basting it with the pan juices every 30 minutes. Then warm the remaining port, pour it over the leg and return the meat to the oven for another 2½ hours.

Remove the meat from the oven and rest it, covered, for at least 20 minutes before carving.

LAMB RUMPS WITH FIG PASTE, ROCKET AND PARMIGIANO REGGIANO SALAD

Serves 2–3

This is a dish that friend and former staff member Victoria Blumenstein liked to cook at the Farmshop, as much as anything to show off our fig paste.

3 quarters preserved lemon, flesh removed, rind rinsed and thinly sliced	500 g milk-fed lamb rumps
⅓ cup (80 ml) verjuice	200 g rocket
145 ml extra virgin olive oil	100 g fig paste, cut into 1 cm cubes
4 sprigs thyme	¼ cup (40 g) pine nuts
2 sprigs French tarragon	80 g Parmigiano Reggiano, shaved
sea salt flakes and freshly ground black pepper	

Soak the preserved lemon in a mixture of 1 tablespoon verjuice and 1 tablespoon water for 30 minutes. To make the resting marinade, combine the remaining verjuice, ½ cup of the olive oil, thyme and tarragon in a glass or ceramic dish, and set aside.

Preheat the oven to 200°C. Season the lamb rumps with salt and pepper, then add the remaining olive oil to a frying pan and seal the rumps over low–medium heat. Transfer to a roasting pan and roast for 15–20 minutes or until cooked to your liking. Remove from the oven, transfer to the marinade and leave for 10–15 minutes.

Toss the rocket, fig paste, pine nuts, Parmigiano Reggiano and preserved lemon together in a bowl. Slice the lamb, then add to the rocket salad, along with a little of the resting juices. Toss gently to combine and serve immediately.

LAMB NECK WITH PRESERVED LEMON, GARLIC AND HERBS *Serves 4*

Although I have given the method for cooking this in a cast-iron casserole in the oven, when I cook this at home I often use a crockpot. For those who wish to do the same, preheat the crockpot on high while preparing the ingredients, then add the olive oil, onions, garlic and herbs and let them get a little colour if time allows. Add the lamb necks and quickly roll them in the onion mixture. Even though the lamb cooks well, the caramelisation of the skin is minimal, so the sealing of the meat with the herbs in a little olive oil before cooking adds greatly to the look and flavour of the dish. Add the preserved lemon, verjuice, stock and pepper, then turn the heat down to low and leave to cook. Eight hours later it's ready to eat. Separate the fat from the juices and then reduce to a sauce consistency; if desired, the olives can be added 10 minutes before the dish is ready to be served.

If you want to let this cook while you're out of the house, and think you may be away for as long as 12 hours, then simply leave out the first portion of cooking over high temperature. If you have any Pickled Quinces (see page 150), then two cored quarters of these added to the pot will go beautifully – the quince will disintegrate, but will add a great flavour.

I like to serve this with boiled waxy potatoes or pumpkin added to the juices. A pan of silverbeet (stalks and all) is a good balance for the rich sweetness of the dish.

⅓ cup (80 ml) extra virgin olive oil
4 onions, quartered
6 cloves garlic, peeled
2 sprigs rosemary
6 small fresh bay leaves
4 sprigs thyme
2 × 700 g lamb necks, each in one piece

2 quarters preserved lemon
100 ml verjuice
2 cups (500 ml) reduced Golden Chicken
    Stock (see page 149)
freshly ground black pepper
16 kalamata olives (optional), pitted

Preheat the oven to 180°C. Choose a cast-iron casserole with a tight-fitting lid that will just hold the lamb necks snugly. Heat the oil in the casserole, then add the onions, garlic and herbs and brown over high heat for a few minutes. Add the lamb necks and roll them to seal in the onion mixture. Add the preserved lemon, verjuice and stock and season with pepper.

Cook, covered, in the oven for 3–5 hours, depending on the quality of the lamb – older lamb will take longer. Skim the fat from the pan juices and reduce the sauce to the desired consistency. Add the olives, if using, then leave to rest for 10 minutes before serving.

BRAISED LAMB LEG WITH ROASTED ROOT VEGETABLES   *Serves 4*

2 cups (500 ml) verjuice

1 cup (250 ml) extra virgin olive oil,
   plus extra for drizzling

2 quarters preserved lemon,
   flesh removed, rind rinsed and diced

1 onion, roughly chopped

1 stick celery, roughly chopped

2 cloves garlic, roughly chopped

4 sprigs rosemary, leaves picked

4 fresh bay leaves

1 × 2.5 kg leg lamb with thigh bone removed

sea salt flakes and freshly ground
   black pepper

2 parsnips, peeled and halved

2 turnips, peeled and halved

1 celeriac, peeled and quartered

4 young carrots, peeled and halved

1 large fennel bulb, trimmed and quartered

1 cup (250 ml) lamb stock *or* Golden
   Chicken Stock (see page 149)

Make a marinade for the lamb by combining 250 ml of the verjuice, the olive oil, preserved lemon, onion, celery, garlic and herbs. Marinate the lamb in this mixture in the refrigerator overnight or for at least 8 hours.

Preheat the oven to 120°C. Place the lamb and marinade in a roasting pan and season. Slowly roast the lamb for 4 hours or until tender, occasionally basting with the marinade. Remove the lamb from the oven and rest it in a warm spot, then turn the oven up to 180°C.

Toss the remaining vegetables in olive oil and season to taste, then place in a shallow roasting pan and roast for about 20 minutes or until tender. Turn the oven temperature up to 200°C, then add the remaining verjuice to the vegetables and return to the oven for another 10 minutes, or until caramelised. Remove from the oven.

In a small saucepan, combine the stock with the juices from the lamb pan and reduce slightly over high heat to form a jus.

Serve the roast vegetables with the sliced lamb and a little jus.

MARINATED BUTTERFLIED LAMB LEG   *Serves 4*

I like to use milk-fed lamb for this recipe, as it is so tender and flavoursome. Ask your butcher to bone and butterfly your leg of lamb, so that it is a neat rectangular shape, or follow the instructions on page 116.

1 × 1.5 kg leg lamb, boned and butterflied

2 cloves garlic, sliced

¼ cup (60 ml) extra virgin olive oil

2 sprigs rosemary, leaves picked

freshly ground black pepper

verjuice, for sprinkling

4 fresh bay leaves

sea salt flakes

RESTING MARINADE

⅓ cup (80 ml) extra virgin olive oil

¼ cup (60 ml) verjuice

2 quarters preserved lemon, flesh removed,
   rind rinsed and finely chopped

3 golden shallots, finely sliced

¼ cup chopped flat-leaf parsley

freshly ground black pepper

Make incisions in the fat of the leg of lamb and insert slices of garlic. Combine the olive oil, rosemary and pepper and rub it well into the lamb in a flat ceramic dish. Sprinkle with verjuice and dot with bay leaves. Leave to marinate for several hours.

When you are ready to cook the meat, mix all the resting marinade ingredients together and pour into a dish large enough to hold the lamb. Set aside.

Preheat both the barbecue grill plate and flat plate to hot. Season the lamb with salt just before cooking. On the grill plate, seal the meat, skin-side down, until it caramelises. Depending on the heat of the grill, this may take a good 5 minutes. Reduce the heat of the flat plate to medium and seal the other side of the meat on the flat plate for 5 minutes. Continue turning the meat on the flat plate until it is cooked, being careful not to burn it; this will take 20–30 minutes, depending on the age of the lamb and how well done you like your meat. If the meat is cooking too fast, wrap it in foil after you have sealed both sides, and finish cooking it in a 180°C oven, if you prefer.

When the meat is cooked to your liking, slip it gently into the resting marinade (after removing the foil, if using) and leave it for a good 15 minutes, turning the meat once during this period.

Serve with sliced red onions grilled on the barbecue and tossed with a little vino cotto, extra virgin olive oil and chopped flat-leaf parsley.

STRAWBERRIES

I FIRST UNDERSTOOD HOW WONDERFUL STRAWBERRIES COULD be when I came across a grower, Bill Gray at Springton, who was so passionate about his produce that in the season he used to drive out to the Pheasant Farm Restaurant every second day to deliver his strawberries. I will never forget the perfume in my office, with 5 kg trays of the most beautiful ripe strawberries you could imagine sitting there. Left to ripen on the stem, then picked early in the morning and driven no more than 20 km, I was getting them at their best. Having them delivered so frequently meant that I never had to refrigerate them, and nothing masks their flavour more than being chilled and thereby picking up other 'fridge' smells; it also toughens their skins. Unfortunately, it got to the stage where people weren't prepared to pay the premium Bill needed to charge to cover the cost of picking the best fruit in perfect condition and, too far from interstate markets to benefit from them, he threw in the towel. The experience of Bill's strawberries has spoilt me forever, and I can no longer bring myself to buy straw-berries in punnets of undeclared picking date, which have been refrigerated and come from who knows where.

Don't think big necessarily means sweet with strawberries (although it can). I am told the best strawberries in the world are the wild strawberries of Europe – the alpine straw-berries, beach strawberries (actually found by the seashore in some parts of the continent) and forest strawberries (the French in particular are passionate about these *fraises des bois*). After 200 years of developing strawberry varieties, it is still these wild strawberries that are supreme in both taste and smell. They are very small and picked very ripe. Plants of alpine strawberries are available in Australia, in particular in South Australia and Victoria, but they have not proved viable for the fresh food market because the demand is for big, colourful fruit that will last.

Strawberry plants look so pretty in a garden, especially when planted along a path. When I had my own plants, I loved to pick a warm, ripe strawberry when arriving home

Moist buttermilk cake with strawberries (see page 131)

at night. The only trouble was that everyone in the family did the same thing, and we then had to buy strawberries from Bill to have enough to make a dessert. When we first moved to our cottage some years ago, all sorts of nooks and crannies were planted with strawberries. The fruit produced was not particularly large, I grant you, but the berries were always delicious, especially when picked and eaten straight from the garden. But then we were invaded by millipedes. After having too many mouthfuls of luscious strawberry spoiled by the skin-crawling crunch of a millipede, I gave up on my plants for many years. However, I have since found runners of smallish, intensely flavoured Japanese strawberries. They are so incredibly sweet it's almost sinful. I'm keen to try growing these, so have planted them in raised beds.

When buying strawberries, there are two things you must be on the lookout for. First, don't be seduced only by the size of the new season's fruit; second, develop a relationship with your greengrocer and find out on which days the strawberries are delivered. If you can get hold of strawberries that have been picked ripe and delivered without any chilling, you will be amazed by the difference in flavour.

How many times have you opened a punnet of strawberries that looked wonderful through the wrapping only to find mouldy berries at the base? The farmer is not trying to trick you; it's just that the fruit has been too long in the fridge. And that first act of chilling really dulls the flavour. However, leaving them out of the fridge also leads to mould.

Strawberries are not often marketed under varietal names, but the practice is increasing as the public becomes more discerning. With a little pressure it may well happen — especially now that more and more keen gardeners are checking out new varieties.

I am a keen but passive member of the Rare Fruit Society SA (www.rarefruit-sa.org.au) and always learn something from their newsletter. Mark Henley, the secretary, carried out trial plantings of six strawberry varieties all sourced through the Rare Fruit Society network. The trial was not without its problems — Mark had to play the 'guess-how-many-millipedes-can-get-into-one-strawberry' game, and had to deal with birds that could spot a strawberry within minutes of it ripening (or so it seemed).

The Aiberry, a bright-red (although not as deep-crimson as some), largish strawberry, won the trial hands down. Mark discovered he could pick this variety just before it was totally ripe and yet the berries were still full of flavour. Those that fully ripened were sweeter than any other he has tasted. Mental note — I must get him to taste my new plantings.

Next year, Mark plans to net the plants and tackle the millipedes whichever way he can. (Whilst I know that coffee grounds deter millipedes, I'm not sure what effect they have on beneficial insects.) He has also offered me runners to plant in May — perhaps one year I'll take the offer up.

Some years ago, a colleague, Di Holuigue, gave me a fascinating little book called *The Compleat Strawberry*, by Stafford Whiteaker. It gives the history of the strawberry and talks about how expensive a treat they were in days gone by. It also details their nutritional aspects. Apparently, strawberries contain large amounts of vitamin C and a high level of fructose, which is more easily assimilated by diabetics than any other type of sugar.

When you have strawberries in perfect condition there is nothing better than a big plateful with fresh cream – the definitive no-nonsense dessert. Another simple treat is to serve them unhulled on a dish with brown sugar and crème fraîche. An interesting accompaniment to strawberries is balsamic vinegar or vino cotto. This is particularly useful when the strawberries are less than perfectly ripe. To a 250 g punnet of strawberries, add 1–2 tablespoons balsamic vinegar or vino cotto to suit individual taste (balsamic vinegar varies in quality and age; the older it is, the more intense and syrupy it will be).

Strawberries can be used for so many desserts – strawberry shortcake, strawberry bread, strawberry tart, and as a filling for sponges. They can be used as a syrup, in a liqueur, as a sauce or a coulis, and to make jam or jellies. Strawberries can be teamed with other flavours such as rhubarb, oranges and raspberries. And pan-fried strawberries in nut-brown butter with freshly ground black pepper, a recipe my friend Ingo Schwartz taught me, really accentuates the strawberry flavour.

STRAWBERRY COULIS
Makes 250 ml

The amount of sugar should reflect the ripeness of the strawberries, so if you are using strawberries that are unripe, pour a little hot sugar syrup over them and leave for a few minutes before blending. To make sugar syrup, heat equal amounts of sugar and water until the sugar has dissolved – for 1 punnet of strawberries, ¼ cup of each should suffice. If you don't want to be bothered making such a small amount of syrup, 1 tablespoon of balsamic vinegar or vino cotto would also help bring out the flavour of the strawberries.

1 × 250 g punnet strawberries   **1 tablespoon castor sugar**

In a blender, purée strawberries and sugar together until liquid. Serve with ice cream or a fruit tart.

MOIST BUTTERMILK CAKE WITH STRAWBERRIES
Serves 8

This cake is very similar to one I made as a prize for a charity fund-raiser – a recipe written especially for the highest bidder. The concept was that the winner would choose the nature of the dish and at first I thought I'd bitten off more than I could chew, as the request was for a first birthday cake. How to make something so familiar different was more of a challenge for me, a person who hardly makes cakes at all, as I wanted it to be a cake that could possibly become a family tradition. I thought long and hard about it and, using my eldest granddaughter Zöe (who was seven at the time) as my critic, I cooked cake after cake for her approval. I sent the recipe on to the winner accompanied by a letter saying how I hoped that this was a cake that the child could make on their own, when they were old enough, and that it could grow as they grew, with different variations on a theme. »

The cake turned out to be such a hit with Zöe, who has a palate like mine and seldom eats cake, but I have altered it slightly to keep the exclusivity of the original recipe.

As, in my experience, everyone fights for the icing, I have been very generous with the quantity so it can be spread thickly over the cake.

butter, for greasing
vegetable oil spray, for greasing
1½ cups (225 g) self-raising flour
1½ teaspoons baking powder
¼ teaspoon salt
1 teaspoon pure vanilla extract
½ cup (125 ml) buttermilk,
    at room temperature
125 g unsalted butter, at room temperature
1¼ cups (275 g) sugar
2 large eggs, at room temperature

3 large egg yolks, at room temperature
finely grated rind of 2 lemons
⅓ cup (80 ml) extra virgin olive oil
really ripe strawberries, to serve

LEMON BUTTER ICING
100 g butter, softened
finely grated rind of 2 lemons
¼ cup (60 ml) lemon juice,
    plus extra to taste
2⅔ cups (430 g) icing sugar, sifted

Preheat the oven to 180°C. Grease an 18 cm cake tin with a little butter, then line with baking paper and lightly spray with vegetable oil.

Sift flour, baking powder and salt together into a bowl. In a separate bowl, add the vanilla extract to the buttermilk. Using an electric mixer, cream the butter on medium speed for 2–3 minutes or until pale, then, with the motor running, add the sugar in a steady stream. If the mixture is not well combined, scrape the sides of the bowl with a rubber spatula and mix for another 3 minutes.

Add the whole eggs, one at a time, and beat for 30 seconds after adding each one. Add the egg yolks, one at a time, and beat for 30 seconds after adding each one. Add the lemon rind, then pour in the oil and mix well with a rubber spatula. Fold in half of the flour mixture, then scrape the sides of the bowl and fold in half of the buttermilk mixture. Fold in the remaining flour, scraping the sides down well, then fold in the remaining buttermilk. Pour the batter into the prepared cake tin.

Bake for about 35 minutes or until the edges begin to come away from the sides of the tin. Cool in the tin for 15 minutes, then invert onto a cooling rack covered with baking paper. Peel the baking paper from the base of the cake, then turn, right-side up, onto another rack. Leave to cool before icing.

For the icing, add the lemon rind and juice and the icing sugar to the butter and stir to combine; add extra lemon juice to taste, as desired. Once the cake is cool, spread it thickly with the icing.

Alternatively, you can leave the cake un-iced and top with really ripe strawberries. It is wonderful sliced and served with a dollop of mascarpone.

DRIED STRAWBERRY BRIOCHE   *Serves 6*

When our daughter Saskia was in her late teens, we bought her a food dehydrator, as she was interested in pursuing her own food production business. Her first effort was dehydrated strawberries, and this marvellous recipe resulted from our wondering what on earth we were going to use them for. Saskia has now gone on to run her own food production business, as well as a catering business with our younger daughter Elli. I wonder if this dehydrator started it all?

1 cup dried strawberries	3 large free-range eggs, beaten
orange liqueur, for soaking	185 g unsalted butter
¼ cup (60 ml) lukewarm water	
7 g dried yeast (or 15 g fresh yeast)	GLAZE
3 teaspoons sugar	1 free-range egg
220 g plain flour	reserved strawberry soaking liquid
1 teaspoon salt	

Place the strawberries in a bowl and cover with orange liqueur to reconstitute.

Pour the lukewarm water into a small bowl and add the yeast and 1 teaspoon of the sugar. Set aside until the yeast dissolves.

Put the flour, remaining 2 teaspoons sugar and the salt into a large bowl and add the yeast mixture and the eggs. Mix by hand, squeezing and pulling the dough upwards, until it becomes elastic. This should take about 20 minutes.

Divide the butter into 6 even pieces and, again using your hands, incorporate the butter into the dough piece by piece. Each new piece should be added only when the last has been absorbed. The dough will be sticky but should retain its elasticity.

Place the dough in a clean bowl, cover with a tea towel and set aside in a draught-free area for about 4 hours to triple its bulk. This is a rich dough that does not need to be in a warm area in order to rise, so if the butter starts to melt and the dough looks oily, place it in the refrigerator from time to time.

Turn the dough onto a lightly floured work surface and shape it into a rectangle. Strain the excess liquid from the strawberries, reserving the liquid, and spread them over the dough. Fold the dough into three, as if you were making puff pastry, then press out again, and again fold it into three. Put the dough back into the bowl, cover, and leave it for about 1½ hours, until it has doubled in volume.

Shape the dough into a round and place it on a plate in the refrigerator for 30 minutes, to make the dough firm enough to shape.

Grease a loaf tin, shape the dough into a sausage and place it in the tin. Set it aside until the dough has doubled in volume (about 1½ hours).

Preheat the oven to 240°C. Make the glaze by beating the egg with the reserved strawberry soaking liquid, then brush over the top of the loaf. Bake for 15 minutes, then reduce the temperature to 200°C and bake for another 30 minutes. Cool on a wire rack.

VEAL

IN MY FIRST FORMAL ITALIAN LESSON, WHEN I ATTEMPTED IN vain to learn the language before my planned cooking school with Stephanie Alexander in Tuscany, the discussion was, of course, about food. 'Italians love to eat veal as they don't like strongly flavoured meat,' my teacher said, which took me aback. I certainly knew they loved veal but I also knew the Italians were just as passionate about game – and what could be stronger in flavour than that?

Don't think of veal as bland, though. It relies on its sweetness and moisture to be special, and can be married with strong Mediterranean flavours – just check your favourite Italian cookbooks for ideas.

In 1995, on my first long stint in Italy, I discovered that eating in local restaurants was not always the paradise I imagined it to be. I should have learnt to stop after the antipasto and pasta, which is fantastic even in the most modest establishments. For my taste, the following meat course was often a disappointment, as I found it overcooked. The exceptions were my beloved offal, and veal. After a while I learnt to play it safe and order a simple piece of pan-fried veal with lemon and sometimes rosemary.

There are few suppliers of milk-fed veal across Australia, as it's a very specialist product and not that easy to obtain, since most butchers sell yearling beef in place of true veal. There is a huge difference between the two, as milk-fed veal is moist, sweet and delicate; to me, yearling occupies a tasteless middle ground between this and the aged beef I like from a mature animal. 'Bobby veal', from unwanted dairy calves, makes a better and easily affordable alternative to yearling.

Milk-fed veal can be fed either mother's milk or formula, but the formula-fed calf takes longer to reach the desired weight than a calf fed by its mother. Age is not so much of an issue with veal as the beast does not have to be tiny for its meat to be tender. The best veal I have ever eaten was at Stephanie's Restaurant during the winter of 1996. I had an enormous veal chop that almost overflowed the plate and was at least a couple of centimetres thick. It was so sweet and succulent I could hardly believe it. I now know that the veal was supplied by Vince and Anne Garreffa's White Rocks Veal in Western Australia, which is still available through Mondo di Carne (www.mondo.net.au). Although White Rocks Veal is a year-round product, most of the choice cuts are pre-sold to a select number of top restaurants. This veal is of a truly amazing quality, so if you ever find yourself in a restaurant where it is on the menu, I recommend that you go for it!

It came as no surprise to me to hear that a young Italian butcher in Myrtleford in Victoria's Ovens Valley is providing veal almost the colour of rabbit (I presume it is milk-fed). There is such a strong Italian community around Myrtleford that many traditions have been kept alive. The Ovens Valley International Festival celebrates this cultural richness in October every second year – a showcase of regional food with a strong Italian influence, which is second to none in Australia to my knowledge.

If you want to give the real thing a go, the best value for money are the leg primals, the muscles that can be cut for quick pan-frying: rump, silverside, round and topside. Slice the meat thinly and give it a little slap with a wooden mallet to tenderise it, then pan-fry it in butter with rosemary, salt, freshly ground black pepper and a squeeze of lemon juice, for a taste of just how delicious veal can be (see page 138).

Veal should be cooked pink but, surprisingly, given the young age of the animal, larger pieces of meat need long, slow cooking to be tender, rather than the fast cooking you might associate with beef or lamb.

A great cut of veal and the most economical of all, other than the shanks, is the shoulder. Cooking on the bone is always best, as it provides sweetness, but there are times when the convenience of carving at the table takes over, and this is one of them. Boned shoulder rolled with a well-seasoned, very moist stuffing (there is so little fat content that you have to work at keeping the moisture in veal) is wonderful and very versatile. Try stuffing the meat with lots of onion sweated in extra virgin olive oil, chopped herbs, bread soaked in milk, and chopped anchovies before rolling and tying it up with string. Rub the shoulder with extra virgin olive oil, rosemary and freshly ground black pepper and wrap it in caul fat to be extra sure that the meat will remain moist. Add a little water to the roasting pan so the juices don't burn during cooking. Cook at 180°C for 20 minutes, then reduce the temperature to 160°C and cook for a further 1½–2 hours – the water and juices will produce a lovely syrupy glaze in the bottom of the pan.

You could add sorrel to the same stuffing, or instead of anchovies, try including a few pitted black olives that have been marinated in a little extra virgin olive oil with grated orange rind and chopped oregano in the stuffing, then rub the shoulder with oregano, olive oil and freshly ground black pepper before roasting.

A leg of veal can of course be prepared and cooked in much the same way. Make pockets to hold the stuffing and use a large piece of caul fat to wrap the leg and hold the stuffing in place. The cooking time will be shorter if you leave the bone in as it acts as a heat conductor – it could make as much as half an hour's difference if cooked at the same temperature as the shoulder.

I love pot-roasting veal shanks. Season and gently brown two shanks on top of the stove in extra virgin olive oil with oregano or rosemary in an enamelled cast-iron casserole and set them aside. Separate a head of garlic, then sauté the cloves in their skins in the same casserole, adding a little more olive oil if necessary. Add wedges of preserved lemon and cook until the garlic begins to soften a little. Deglaze the pan with white wine or verjuice, then add some veal or chicken stock. Return the meat to the casserole, then cover it with a tight-fitting lid and bake in the oven at 180°C for 30 minutes. Turn the shanks over and see if they need any more stock. Turn the oven down to 120°C and cook for another hour, then check the level of the stock and test whether the meat is nearly done – the shanks are ready when the meat begins to come away from the bone and a gelatinous syrup has formed. (Larger shanks may need another 30 minutes.) You could also add a handful of sorrel to the pan in the last 10 minutes of cooking – it will become a purée and add another dimension to the sauce.

The Pheasant Farm Restaurant menu often featured two rather extravagant veal 'sandwiches'. For the first, I deep-fried long, thin slices of eggplant in extra virgin olive oil and then drained them and lightly dressed them with more of the oil, basil, balsamic vinegar, salt and freshly ground black pepper. I then made an aïoli, thick and luscious but with a good bit of lemon juice in it. Next I pan-fried several thin pieces of veal in nut-brown butter. The veal, eggplant (with dressing and basil) and aïoli were layered, finishing with veal and eggplant. A handful of rocket was served alongside, 'dressed' by the juices that oozed out over the plate. Sometimes we would spoon a little of this jus over the top of the sandwich so that it mingled with the dressing and the aïoli.

The second we served in autumn, when we would sauté fresh figs and slices of meyer lemon in lots of butter and freshly ground black pepper and pan-fry the veal with rosemary. Assembled the same way as the other 'sandwich', this dish was served with a lemon mayon-naise and rocket.

I remember the first time I made *vitello tonnato*. It was quite an occasion, since it used to be almost impossible to get proper veal, and this was also the first time I'd found good local capers. For once in my life I followed a recipe to the letter and, thrilled with the outcome, I put the dish on the menu. There were no instructions for carving the veal in the Italian cookbook I was using, so I followed my instincts and preference for generosity. The result was a plate of quite hearty slices of succulent veal that I thought a triumph, blanketed as they were by the tuna mayonnaise. The first customer to try it was something of an Italophile, and condescendingly sent a message back to the kitchen saying the *vitello tonnato* was incorrect as the meat should have been thinly sliced. My confidence was bruised somewhat, but I heeded the advice and used thinly sliced veal from then on, with great success.

VITELLO TONNATO   *Serves 6*

I first came across this method for cooking *vitello tonnato* in Ada Boni's *Italian Regional Cooking*, and the following recipe is my adaptation of it. Poaching the veal the day before will really enhance the flavours. The trick to making the mayonnaise for this dish is to first make it super-thick by adding the oil very slowly, so that when you add the puréed mixture, it thins it to the right consistency.

While I've recommended using tinned Italian tuna here, I'm always hopeful that we'll soon see good-quality Australian tuna in olive oil on our supermarket shelves.

2 × 350 g pieces nut of veal

1 onion, finely chopped

2 × 95 g tins Italian tuna in olive oil, drained

2 fresh bay leaves

1 × 45 g tin of anchovies, drained

2 tablespoons capers

1 cup (250 ml) extra virgin olive oil

1½ cups (375 ml) verjuice *or* dry white wine

2 hard-boiled egg yolks

1 egg yolk

sea salt flakes and freshly ground
   black pepper

squeeze of lemon juice

1 lemon, thinly sliced

12 tiny cornichons (see Glossary)

Put the veal into a heavy-based saucepan or enamelled cast-iron casserole just large enough to take all the ingredients, so as to minimise the amount of liquid required. Cover the veal with the onion, tuna, bay leaves, 2 anchovy fillets and half of the capers. Tip in 75 ml of the olive oil, the verjuice or dry white wine and up to 375 ml water, adding just enough liquid to immerse the veal during cooking. Bring to a simmer, then cover, reduce the heat to low and cook at a gentle simmer for 1 hour (control the heat by using a simmer mat if necessary). Remove the pan from the heat and allow the meat to cool completely in its juices.

Once cooled, remove the meat and set aside, discarding the bay leaves. Strain the cooking liquid, reserving both the solids and liquid. Purée the solids with 250 ml of the strained cooking liquid using a sieve or food mill (or blend it in a food processor and then sieve it). Set aside. Reserve the remaining strained liquid to use as a light stock when making a risotto.

Using a mortar and pestle, smash the hard-boiled egg yolks to a paste with a dash of lemon juice, then add the raw egg yolk (this could also be done carefully in a food processor). Slowly add the remaining olive oil drop by drop, incorporating it into the mixture as you go, then add 250 ml of the sieved sauce. Check for seasoning and acidity, adding more lemon juice if required.

Slice the veal very thinly, making sure you cut across the grain, and overlap the slices on a platter like roof tiles. Cover the meat with the mayonnaise, then arrange the remaining anchovies, cut into strips, in a criss-cross pattern and place the remaining capers in the centre of each 'diamond'. Serve at room temperature with thinly sliced lemon and cornichons. If made the day before and refrigerated, then removed from the fridge to come to room temperature, the flavour of this dish will be enhanced.

VEAL PAN-FRIED WITH ROSEMARY AND LEMON *Serves 4*

8 thin slices veal, cut from the leg
   (about 500 g)
100 g butter
2 tablespoons rosemary leaves
extra virgin olive oil, for cooking

sea salt flakes and freshly ground
   black pepper
75 g (½ cup) plain flour
1½ tablespoons lemon juice

Gently pat the veal with a wooden mallet. Heat half the butter in a frying pan with half the rosemary and cook gently over low heat until the butter is nut-brown, adding a splash of extra virgin olive oil to inhibit burning, then remove from the heat for a moment. Season the flour, then dust the veal with it and shake off the excess.

Adjust the heat to medium, return the pan to the heat and cook 2 slices of veal at a time so that the meat doesn't poach rather than fry. Gently seal for about a minute, then flip over and seal the other side. Remove the veal from the pan and keep it warm while you cook the next 2 slices of meat, then deglaze the pan with half the lemon juice and tip the

Vitello tonnato (see page 137)

juices over the resting meat. Cook the remaining rosemary with the balance of the butter until the butter is nut-brown, add some olive oil as previously, then pan-fry the next 2 batches of veal. Deglaze the pan with the last of the lemon juice and, using a spatula, add the contents of the pan to the resting veal. Serve the veal immediately, with the pan juices, a salad of bitter greens and a dish of steaming mashed potato.

CALF'S LIVER WITH SAGE   *Serves 2*

I'm such an offal freak that I can't bear not to include a liver dish here, even if this chapter is about veal. To my mind, veal or calf's liver is the best part of the animal. In the early days of the restaurant I was told that sweetbreads and calf's liver were either exported or taken home by the abattoir workers. Things have changed somewhat but it's still quite difficult to get fresh calf's liver: find a passionate butcher, order it in advance and make sure you cook it the day it comes in.

30 sage leaves
100 g butter
sea salt flakes and freshly ground
   black pepper

plain flour, for dusting
6 thin slices calf's liver (about 250 g)
dash good balsamic vinegar *or*
   vino cotto (see Glossary), optional

Cook the sage leaves and butter over low heat in a frying pan until the butter is nut-brown. Season the flour, then dust the liver with it. Gently cook 2 slices of liver at a time for about 1 minute, then flip them over and seal the other side. Keep the cooked liver warm while you seal the next batch. Make sure that the butter remains nut-brown and the sage leaves are crisp but not burnt – you may need to adjust the temperature. Pour off any excess butter and, if desired, deglaze the pan with a splash of balsamic vinegar or vino cotto. Serve the liver and sage leaves immediately, along with any pan juices.

VINE LEAVES

WHILE I NOW HAVE A BIT OF A THING FOR WRAPPING FOOD IN vine leaves, I regret the years of lost opportunity when I didn't use them for this purpose. I have had masses of vine leaves at my disposal since we moved to the Barossa in 1973 but my dislike of dolmades, with their tea-leaf flavour and rice filling, kept me away from them.

It was, in fact, my first trip to Bali in the mid-1980s that turned me around. There I delighted in fish wrapped in banana leaves with fragrant spices. I tried to grow a banana palm on my return home, against every law of nature considering our Mediterranean climate, but as it was just the leaf I was after I thought it worth taking a chance. It didn't work. I then became similarly intrigued by lotus leaves after an amazing meal cooked by Phillip Searle, then at Oasis Seros, at the fourth Symposium of Gastronomy in Sydney. He had stuffed boned quail with lots of bone marrow, pancetta and black rice flavoured with strangely piquant yet desirable fish sauce (it was so sticky and unctuous I can taste it now), then wrapped them in lotus leaves. He rolled out a piece of clay and made individual sarcophagi for the quail, which he then baked.

However, I finally gave in to the climate and gave up my ideas of the exotic. Vine leaves are now indispensable to me – and I can't understand my earlier rejection of them. Sometimes life can be so busy that you don't see or appreciate the wealth around you, even if you're food-obsessed like me. It was, for example, my friend Stephanie Alexander, who has taught me so much over the years through her writing, her cooking and, even better, her visits, who suggested I tried blanching vine tendrils early in the season to add an almost asparagus-like flavour to salads (pumpkin tendrils are also worthy of the same treatment, I've since discovered). I had never thought to use these before – yet, like vine leaves, they were quite literally on my doorstep. And I now know that it's all in the way you prepare them – the 'tea leaf' taste I hated so much about vine leaves can be easily avoided.

I use fresh young leaves in the spring just as they are. Most cookbooks suggest you blanch fresh vine leaves in water before use, but this isn't necessary if you have access to very young leaves (always assuming the vigneron isn't berating you for pinching too much of the canopy). Just wash them to remove any sprays and wrap them around the food as they are. Although I love the principle of putting produce aside to use in the winter, I have to admit that I never manage to preserve my own vine leaves for long-term storage. I keep a jar of vine leaves preserved in brine or vacuum-packed vine leaves as a backup, but these do require a fair bit of soaking to rid them of excess salt.

I thought of using wine for cooking older leaves in, then I extended the idea and cooked both the leaves and tendrils in verjuice. They were exquisite! My first experiment with vine leaves cooked in verjuice featured tiny yabbies from our dam. They were too small to make a significant dish – there had been a drought for several years and the yabbies had not grown to any size – so I cooked and peeled them, then wrapped each in a vine leaf and pan-fried them quickly in nut-brown butter. Served with a glass of four-year-old Barossa semillon, these were a heady combination.

Cooking vine leaves in verjuice is an easy way to preserve them for short-term storage. All you need do is bring verjuice to the boil and slip the leaves in, one at a time. Young leaves will take about a minute, while older leaves may take up to 3 minutes. Once they are poached, store them in a glass container and tip in fresh verjuice to cover them. The leaves lose their vibrant green colour but make up for it in flavour. The pH level of verjuice is not as low as that of vinegar but I have still found it suitable for keeping the vine leaves, refrigerated, for several months. The addition of a little salt, sprinkled between the leaves, would be an extra precaution. The verjuice-poached leaves, drained and dried, can be dotted with butter and baked at 220°C for 2 minutes to crisp up just like a sage leaf. I serve these alongside grilled quail.

I have now tackled dolmades again, and have come up with a simplified version that will probably make traditionalists tut-tut. I suggest you cook the rice the way you like it and then add your favourite flavourings. The Moorish influence found in Sicilian cooking suits me best of all: rice with lots of caramelised onion, currants, pine nuts, preserved lemon and fennel fronds or mint leaves. Wrap a little of the rice in each blanched vine leaf, then put the bundles into a dish, brush them with extra virgin olive oil and they're ready to eat – with none of the cooking that traditional dolmades require! As I prefer these 'dolmades' served warm, I put the dish into a 180°C oven for about 10 minutes.

Wrapping vine leaves around small game birds for grilling or baking is a very traditional practice in Italy and France, and is particularly successful with quail, partridge and baby chicken, as the leaves are just the right size to protect the breast. Small fish, such as red mullet or fresh sardines, are great done this way too. Brush the parcels with olive oil and squeeze some lemon juice over before grilling for just a few minutes for sardines, and up to 6 minutes for red mullet (if baking, do so at 230°C for a similar length of time). Grilling will render the leaves more brittle but the contents will still be protected and the leaves, though charred, will be edible. I love the smoky, grapey flavour the leaves impart.

You don't have to limit yourself to using small fish or fowl with vine leaves, however. You can also wrap a boned and stuffed chicken or a large fish. Arrange a 'sheet' of blanched vine leaves, overlapped like roof tiles, then carefully wrap it around the chicken or fish. If you are using fish and grapes are in season, try stuffing the cavity with seedless green grapes, breadcrumbs, lots of fresh herbs, and onion sweated until almost caramelised. A 3 kg fish may take 35 minutes to cook at 220°C, while a large boned fowl (say 2.5 kg) will take 45–55 minutes – both need to be turned halfway through the cooking.

CULTIVATED MUSHROOMS IN VINE LEAVES WITH VERJUICE *Serves 6*

The original inspiration for this dish was a recipe in Elizabeth David's *An Omelette and a Glass of Wine*. I served this dish in the restaurant as an accompaniment to rabbit in particular, when wild mushrooms were not in season and I wanted to add an earthiness to the dish that cultivated mushrooms couldn't provide. Vine leaves give a wonderful dimension to these mushrooms – it is as if you have picked your own from the paddock. My version uses vine leaves blanched in verjuice.

6 cloves garlic

150 ml extra virgin olive oil

200 ml verjuice

12 fresh young vine leaves

300 g (about 12) flat cultivated mushrooms

sea salt flakes and freshly ground
   black pepper

Preheat the oven to 200°C. In a small frying pan, slowly caramelise the garlic cloves in 1 tablespoon of the olive oil over low heat. Bring the verjuice to the boil in an enamelled or stainless steel saucepan, then blanch the vine leaves by immersing them one at a time into the hot liquid, then drain well. Reserve the verjuice.

Line a small ovenproof dish with 6 of the vine leaves. Drizzle with a little more of the olive oil, then arrange a layer of mushrooms, followed by the garlic, a pinch of salt and a turn of the pepper grinder, then another drizzle of the oil. Add another layer of mushrooms and repeat the procedure. Top with the remaining vine leaves and drizzle over the last of the olive oil. Bake for 25 minutes. While still hot, drizzle 2 tablespoons of the reserved verjuice over the dish to create a vinaigrette. Both the leaves and the mushrooms are eaten – and any leftovers are very good refrigerated for the next day.

VINE LEAVES FILLED WITH GOAT'S CHEESE AND WALNUTS   *Serves 4*

You can grill these on the barbecue or chargrill plate as an alternative to baking.

12 shelled walnuts

200 ml verjuice

12 fresh young vine leaves

2 tablespoons flat-leaf parsley leaves

300 g fresh goat's cheese

walnut oil, for brushing

sea salt flakes and freshly ground
   black pepper

Preheat the oven to 220°C. Dry-roast the walnuts on a baking tray for 6–8 minutes, then rub off their skins with a clean tea towel. Bring the verjuice to the boil in an enamelled or stainless steel saucepan, blanch the vine leaves by immersing them one at a time into the hot liquid, then drain well. Reserve the verjuice.

Roughly chop the walnuts and parsley and mix them into the goat's cheese. Form the cheese into a log (if too soft, refrigerate it to firm it up a bit). Cut the log into 12 even pieces and wrap each in a vine leaf. Brush each parcel with walnut oil, then season and bake for 4 minutes to warm the goat's cheese. Make a vinaigrette with walnut oil and some of the reserved verjuice and spoon it over the warmed parcels. Serve with crusty bread.

BASICS

SORREL MAYONNAISE

2 egg yolks

1 cup trimmed sorrel

pinch salt

juice of ½ lemon

½ cup (125 ml) mellow extra virgin olive oil

½ cup (125 ml) grapeseed oil

freshly ground black pepper

There is no need to chop the sorrel if you are using a blender, though you may need to if using a mortar and pestle. Blend the egg yolks with the sorrel and salt, then add a squeeze of lemon juice. When amalgamated, pour in the combined oils very slowly with the motor running until the mixture becomes very thick. Add a little more lemon juice, if required, and grind in some pepper, then continue pouring in the oil (it can go in a little faster at this stage). When the mayonnaise has emulsified, check whether any extra lemon juice or seasoning is required.

ANCHOVY MAYONNAISE

Try this with poussins that have been barbecued, roasted or poached in stock. I also love it with barbecued kangaroo or pan-fried lamb's brains, but most of all, with veal or rabbit scaloppine.

2–3 anchovy fillets, chopped

2 egg yolks

2 teaspoons Dijon mustard

3 teaspoons white-wine vinegar

1 cup (250 ml) mellow extra virgin olive oil
or half olive and half vegetable oil

sea salt flakes and freshly ground
black pepper

Blend the anchovy fillets in a food processor or blender with the egg yolks, mustard and vinegar for 4–5 seconds or until incorporated. With the motor running, slowly pour in the oil in a thin and steady stream until the mayonnaise thickens and emulsifies. The trick is to do it slowly, so that the mayonnaise doesn't split. Season with salt and pepper and add a dash of hot water to thin and stabilise the mayonnaise, if necessary.

MAYONNAISE

Homemade mayonnaise adds so much to a meal, with very little effort involved. The technique is really very simple (and even a split mayonnaise can be resurrected by starting again in a clean, dry bowl, with fresh egg yolks, before incorporating the split mixture drop by drop).

A basic mayonnaise consists of olive oil, egg yolks, some seasoning and an acidulant such as lemon juice, verjuice or vinegar. I use a mixture of half extra virgin olive oil and half a lighter vegetable or grapeseed oil (this is the one exception I make to my rule about only using extra virgin, as the flavour can be too sharp). The quality of the eggs will have a bearing on the final dish, so free-range eggs at room temperature are best. Mustard is often included but is optional, while salt, I think, is essential. Mayonnaise is at its silkiest when made by hand, but it can also be made successfully in a blender or food processor. Or, you could start using a machine and finish by hand to achieve that 'almost as good as handmade' effect.

Mayonnaise goes with almost every type of meat and fish (particularly when barbecued), not to mention vegetables and salads. Once you master a basic mayonnaise you can use your imagination to change the texture, flavour and colour. Depending on the dish with which the mayonnaise is to be served, you can experiment with verjuice or wine vinegar as the acidulant. Try adding herbs – lemon thyme mayonnaise is great with snapper, and give Sorrel Mayonnaise (see page 147) a go. Garlic mayonnaise (or Aïoli, see page 49) can be made by adding raw garlic, or puréed roasted garlic for a mellower, nuttier flavour. Rouille (see page 48), essentially an aïoli with puréed roasted capsicum, is wonderful added to a fish soup and is simple to make once you are confident with the technique. I serve roasted garlic and quince mayonnaise with kid pot-roasted with lemon, fresh herbs and garlic, so, as you can see, the combinations are endless.

2 large free-range egg yolks	½ cup (125 ml) extra virgin olive oil
(at room temperature)	½ cup (125 ml) vegetable *or* grapeseed oil
pinch sea salt flakes	freshly ground black pepper
1 tablespoon lemon juice	1 tablespoon boiling water (if necessary)
1 teaspoon Dijon mustard (optional)	

Rinse a bowl with hot water and dry thoroughly. Whisk the egg yolks in the bowl with a pinch of salt until thick, then add two-thirds of the lemon juice and the mustard, if using, and whisk until smooth. Continue to whisk whilst adding the oil slowly, drop by drop to begin with. Once the mixture begins to thicken you can add the remaining oil in a slow, steady stream, whisking continuously. When all the oil has been added, taste and add as much of the remaining lemon juice as needed. Season with pepper, and add more salt and lemon juice if needed. Only add the boiling water if the mayonnaise needs thinning and requires no more acidulant.

GOLDEN CHICKEN STOCK

Makes about 2 litres

I just can't cook without a good stock, and a chook stock is the one I use most of all. While there are a few good stocks on the market, usually made by small producers (ourselves included), for me nothing touches the homemade.

The better the quality of the original chook the better your stock will be. The skin and bones (with a generous amount of meat still attached) of a mature, well-brought-up bird has not only better flavour but more gelatinous quality. It's truly important not to overcook a stock; your benchmark should be that the meat on the bones is still sweet. An overcooked stock has all the goodness cooked out of it, and the bones have a chalky flavour.

I tend to make my stock in a large batch and then freeze it in 1-litre containers. Using fresh 'bright' vegetables rather than limp leftovers, and roasting the bones and veg before simmering them, gives the stock a wonderful golden colour and a deeper flavour. You only need use enough water to cover the bones and veg by about 7 cm in your stockpot (this way in most cases your stock won't need reducing). Never allow your stock to boil, just bring it to a good simmer, and don't skim it as you'll take the fat – and the flavour – off with it (you can remove the fat easily after the cooked stock has been refrigerated.) Don't let the stock sit in the pan once it is cooked: strain it straight away, then let it cool before refrigerating.

1 large boiling chicken (about 2.2 kg), cut
    into pieces (if you are using bones only,
    you will need 3 kg)
2 large onions, unpeeled and halved
1 large carrot, roughly chopped
extra virgin olive oil, for cooking
100 ml white wine (optional)
1 large leek, trimmed, cleaned and
    roughly chopped

1 stick celery, roughly chopped
1 bay leaf
6 sprigs thyme
6 stalks flat-leaf parsley
1 head garlic, halved widthways
2 very ripe tomatoes, roughly chopped

Preheat the oven to 200°C. Place the chicken pieces, onion and carrot in a roasting pan and drizzle with a little olive oil. Roast for 20 minutes or until chicken and vegetables are golden brown. »

Transfer the chicken and vegetables to a large stockpot, then deglaze the roasting pan with wine over high heat, if using. Add the wine with the remaining vegetables and herbs to the pot, and cover with about 2.5 litres water. Simmer, uncovered, for 3–4 hours.

Strain the stock straight away through a sieve into a bowl, then cool by immersing the bowl in a sink of cold water. Refrigerate the stock to let any fat settle on the surface, then remove the fat.

The stock will keep for up to 4 days in the refrigerator or for 3 months in the freezer. To reduce the stock, boil in a saucepan over high heat until it is reduced by three-quarters. When the reduced stock is chilled in the refrigerator, it should set as a jelly; if not, reduce again. Jellied stock will keep in the refrigerator for 2–3 days, and in the freezer for 3 months.

FLO BEER'S PICKLED QUINCES

Flo Beer, my very special mother-in-law, shared this recipe with me the first time Colin took me home to Mallala to meet his family, only three weeks before our wedding – 45 years ago now. As a lover of pickles, I never miss making a batch every year, and I think of her every time. They are wonderful with ham and terrines or grilled meats, particularly duck or game. Adding some of the juices to a beef or poultry sauce, which is then reduced to a glaze, also works brilliantly.

This recipe is written to work equally well for those who have bought a kilo of quinces from the greengrocer and those wondering what to do with boxes and boxes of the fruit. The volume of liquid required is enough to just cover the cut quinces. You can establish this at the beginning by covering the cut quinces with water, measuring the water used, and using this amount of vinegar.

quinces	**castor sugar**
lemon juice	**whole cloves**
white-wine vinegar (the better the quality, the better the final product)	**black peppercorns**

Wash, peel and core the quinces and cut into quarters or eighths, depending on the size, retaining the skins and cores. Put the cut quinces immediately into water to which lemon juice has been added, to prevent discolouration.

For each 600 ml vinegar, add 440 g sugar, 1 teaspoon cloves and 1 teaspoon peppercorns. Heat the vinegar in a large heavy-based saucepan, then pour in the sugar in a stream to dissolve. Bring to the boil, then add the cloves and peppercorns and boil rapidly to begin forming a syrup. Turn the heat down to low and cook for 15 minutes.

Place the reserved peels and cores in a muslin bag and add to the syrup; it will immediately take on a rosy glow. Add the sliced quinces and cook for about 15 minutes or until they have turned pink and are soft but not mushy.

Store in clean airtight jars with the quinces well-immersed in the liquid. The colour of the quinces will deepen in the jar. Leave for several weeks before opening.

SALSA AGRESTO

1 cup (160 g) almonds
1 cup (100 g) walnuts
2 cloves garlic
2 ¾ cups flat-leaf parsley leaves
½ cup firmly packed basil leaves

1 ½ teaspoons sea salt flakes
freshly ground pepper
¾ cup (180 ml) extra virgin olive oil
¾ cup (180 ml) verjuice

Preheat the oven to 200°C. Roast the almonds and walnuts on separate baking trays for about 5 minutes, shaking to prevent burning. Rub walnuts in a tea towel to remove bitter skins, then leave to cool. Blend the nuts, garlic, herbs, salt and 6 grinds of black pepper in a food processor with a little of the olive oil. With the motor running, slowly add the remaining oil and verjuice last. The consistency should be like pesto. (If required, thin with more verjuice.)

SOUR-CREAM PASTRY

This recipe makes a very short, flaky pastry with a light, melt-in-the-mouth texture. It is a great all-rounder and can be used in a whole variety of dishes, both sweet and savoury. I like to chill the pastry case in the freezer, as this ensures it is really well-chilled before it goes in the oven.

This pastry rises beautifully and is really light and flaky, which is great if you're making a tart or a pie, but if you want a flat pastry, like a thin pizza dough, a good trick is to 'inhibit' the pastry as it cooks. To do this, carefully open the oven halfway through the cooking (when the pastry is beginning to rise), take out the tray for a moment and press down on the pastry with a similar-sized tray or a clean tea towel, then return the tray to the oven. This will stop the pastry rising too much.

200 g chilled unsalted butter, chopped into
small pieces

250 g plain flour
120 g sour cream

Put the butter and flour into the bowl of a food processor, then pulse until the mixture resembles coarse breadcrumbs. Add the sour cream and pulse again until the dough just forms a ball. If shrinkage worries you, gather the dough into a ball with your hands and bounce it on the bench. Carefully wrap the dough in plastic film and leave to rest in the refrigerator for 15–20 minutes.

Roll out the dough until it is 5 mm thick, then use it to line a 20 cm tart tin with a removable base. Chill the pastry case for 20 minutes.

To blind bake, preheat the oven to 200°C. Line the pastry case with foil, then cover with pastry weights. Blind bake the pastry case for 15 minutes, then remove the foil and pastry weights and bake for another 5 minutes.

FRESH PASTA

About 500 g fresh pasta will serve four adults as a main course. The dough should be tight but malleable. If it becomes too loose, it will still be suitable for making ravioli.

500 g strong flour (see Glossary)	**4 × 61 g eggs**
1 teaspoon salt	**1–2 egg yolks (depending on the flour)**

Mix the flour with the salt, then spread it out into a circle 30 cm in diameter over a clean work surface. Hollow out the centre, leaving just a bank of flour around the edges. Break the eggs into the well, then add the yolks. Using one hand, whisk the eggs and yolks until they're amalgamated, and then, using a fork held in the other hand, scoop the flour a little at a time from the 'banks' into the egg mixture, still whisking with one hand. Keep doing this until the mixture becomes a paste.

Scrape up the dough, 'cutting' it until the mixture is well combined. This involves gathering the mass and smearing it across the bench with the pastry scraper until it all comes together. The dough should then be kneaded for 6–10 minutes, pushing the dough away from you with the heel of your hand, then turning it a quarter to the right, folding the dough over, pushing it away and so on.

Once the dough is shiny and silky, roll it into a ball and wrap it in plastic film. Rest it in the refrigerator for 30 minutes.

Set the pasta machine on a bench, screwing it down firmly. Cut the dough into 10 even pieces and cover with a tea towel. Working in batches, take one piece of dough and press it as flat as you can with the palm of your hand, then feed it through the rollers set on their widest aperture. Fold the rolled dough in thirds, and then pass the narrow end through the machine again. Repeat several times, preferably until you hear a sound that I can only describe as a 'plop' – this is the tension of the dough releasing as it goes through the rollers.

Adjust the machine to the next setting and pass the dough through. Repeat this with every setting until you get to the second to last. As the dough moves through each setting it will become finer and finer and the sheets will become longer and longer; you may need to cut the sheets to make them more manageable.

Unless I'm making ravioli, where I want the pasta to be almost diaphanous, I'll stop at the second to last setting, then adjust the machine, adding the cutters, and run the pasta through the cutters. If I'm making long pasta, I like to have someone help here. Hang the pasta ribbons over the back of a chair or a broom handle to dry.

When ready to cook, bring a large saucepan of water to the boil and add a generous amount of salt. Tip in the pasta and cook until done, testing a strand after 3 minutes. Have a large colander at the ready in the sink, strain the pasta and tip it back into the pan (you may also want to save a little of the cooking water, in case you need it to bind the sauce). Don't rinse the pasta or you'll lose the starch that helps the sauce or oil adhere. If you're not ready to use it immediately, spread out the pasta on a large tray to cool drizzled with extra virgin olive oil – I hate to admit it, but it reheats beautifully in the microwave.

PLUM SAUCE

This is my interpretation of one of the many recipes for plum sauce in *The Barossa Cookery Book*, first published in 1917. This sauce is marvellous with barbecued pork sausages or grilled duck or kangaroo fillets.

3 kg blood plums

1 × 60 g piece ginger

500 g onions, roughly chopped

2 cloves garlic, sliced

extra virgin olive oil, for cooking

1.25 kg sugar

2 cups (500 ml) red-wine vinegar

2 teaspoons black peppercorns

½ teaspoon cayenne pepper

Halve the plums, leaving the stones intact. Bruise the ginger by pressing down on it with the flat blade of a knife. Sauté the onion, garlic and ginger in a little olive oil in a large preserving pan until softened. Add the remaining ingredients and cook for about 30 minutes or until the plum stones come away from the flesh. Strain the sauce and leave to cool. Fill hot sterilised bottles (see Glossary) with the cooled sauce and seal.

LIST OF SOURCES

The author and publisher would like to thank the following people and companies for allowing us to reproduce their material in this book. In some cases we were not able to contact the copyright owners; we would appreciate hearing from any copyright holders not acknowledged here, so that we can properly acknowledge their contribution when this book is reprinted.

Extracts
Pellegrini, Angelo M., *The Food Lover's Garden*, Lyons & Burford, New York, 1970; Waters, Alice, *Chez Panisse Cafe Cookbook*, Random House, New York, 1999.

Recipes
Cheong Liew's salt water duck accompanied by asparagus: Cheong Liew; Stephanie's honey and lavender ice cream, Stephanie Alexander; Janni's braised artichokes with artichoke puree: Janni Kyritsis; Peter Wall's lamb, barley and cinnamon casserole: Peter Wall.

GLOSSARY

Wherever possible, I've explained any less familiar ingredients and techniques in the relevant recipes, but I've also included brief notes here on some ingredients and procedures that are used throughout the book.

Caul fat (*crépine*)
This is the lining of a pig's stomach, and can be used to wrap cuts of meat or delicate food such as kidneys before baking or pan-frying, to help retain moisture and add flavour.

You'll need to order caul fat in advance from your butcher.

Cheese
see Labna; Parmigiano Reggiano

Chocolate
The flavour of chocolate is determined by the amounts of chocolate liquor and cocoa solids it contains.

Bitter chocolate has the highest percentage of cocoa liquor and no added sugar, so it has a strong chocolate flavour, which adds depth to savoury dishes.

A good bittersweet chocolate may contain 65–70 per cent cocoa solids, and the best even more. Because it has sugar added, it is mostly used for sweet dishes – or eating.

Couverture chocolate is the name given to high-quality chocolate that melts well and dries to a glossy finish, making it perfect for covering cakes and for making fine desserts. It can also be used in any recipe calling for chocolate, since its high cocoa butter content gives it a fine flavour and texture.

Cornichons
Cornichons are tiny, crisp gherkins pickled in the French manner: picked when they are 3–8 cm long, and pickled in vinegar or brine. They are crunchy and salty, and are perfect to serve with rillettes, pâtés or terrines, to accompany a charcuterie plate, or as part of a ploughman's lunch.

Cream
In Australia, most cows are kept to produce milk rather than cream, so the fat content of their milk needs to be supplemented at various times of the year to bring it up to the 35 per cent fat content that is needed for pure cream. With nothing else added, this cream is good for enriching sauces.

Any cream labelled 'thickened cream' also has a thickener such as gelatine added. Because of the extra stability that the thickener provides, this is the best cream for whipping – just remember that reduced-fat thickened cream (with around 18 per cent fat) cannot be whipped successfully.

Double cream is very rich, with a fat content of 45–60 per cent. Some of the thicker ones are perfect for spooning alongside a dessert. Try to find farmhouse versions that have been separated from unhomogenised milk.

Flour
Strong flour, also known as bread flour or baker's flour, is my staple flour. What differentiates strong flour is its high gluten content, which allows dough to stretch rather than break during kneading and

rolling, making it particularly suitable for making pasta and bread. The gluten in strong flour also helps to ensure an extensive and even rise in bread.

Flours are further classified according to the percentage of wheat grain present. Wholemeal flour contains the whole grain, and so has a wonderful nutty taste, while brown flour contains about 85 per cent of the grain and white flour between 75 and 80 per cent. The flour industry is moving to predominantly unbleached flour; bleached flour must be specially requested. I prefer unbleached flour as it contains slightly more nutrients; it also has a more robust texture, which works well in breads and pizza bases.

Self-raising flour is plain flour with baking powder and salt added during the milling process, in the proportions of about 1¼ teaspoons of baking powder and a pinch of salt for every cup of flour.

It is used for making pancakes, cakes and muffins.

Gelatine

Gelatine leaves have a better flavour and texture than powdered gelatine. However, confusion can arise from the fact that the gelling strength of gelatine leaves is measured by their 'bloom' rather than their weight. All my recipes have been developed using Alba brand Gold-strength leaves, which weigh 2 g each and have a bloom of 190–220 g.

As gelatine will set more firmly over time, you may be able to use less gelatine if you can make the jelly the day before it is needed. A couple of other things to note: gelatine takes twice as long to dissolve in cream or milk as it does in water; and sugar can inhibit setting, so the higher the sugar content, the softer the set will be.

Labna

Also referred to as yoghurt cheese, labna in its purest form is simply thick drained yoghurt. You can make it yourself by stirring 5 g salt into 500 ml plain yoghurt (the kind with no pectin, gums or other stabilisers) then placing it in a sieve lined with muslin or a clean Chux and leaving it to drain for at least 4 hours or overnight – the longer you leave it, the thicker it will get. Commercial labna is tart and tangy: some versions are thick enough to hold up a spoon, while others are more like soft sour cream.

Parmigiano Reggiano

Authentic aged parmesan cheese made in Italy according to specific traditional practices, Parmigiano Reggiano is my first choice for use in risottos, polenta, soups, and sauces such as pesto. I also love it as part of a cheese board or freshly shaved in salads. Grana Padano has a similar flavour to Parmigiano Reggiano, but has not been aged for as long, so can be a useful, less expensive alternative.

Sugar syrup

Sugar syrup is a simple solution of 1 part sugar dissolved in 1–2 parts water (depending on its intended use) over low heat. It is great to have on hand if you are keen on whipping up your own cocktails at home!

Sterilising jars and bottles

To sterilise jars that are to be used for storing or preserving food, wash the jars and lids in hot, soapy water, then rinse them in hot water and place them in a 120°C oven for approximately 15 minutes to dry out. This method also works for bottles.

Vino cotto

Literally meaning 'cooked wine' in Italian, this traditional Italian preparation is made by simmering unfermented grape juice until it is reduced to a syrup. The one I produce is finished with traditional red-wine vinegar to make it truly *agrodolce* (sweet–sour). With a much softer flavour than vinegar, vino cotto can be used to make sauces for meat or salad dressings or even drizzled over strawberries. In fact, it can be used anywhere you would normally use balsamic vinegar.

BIBLIOGRAPHY

Alexander, Stephanie, *The Cook's Companion* (2nd edition), Lantern, Melbourne, 2004.

—— *Cooking and Travelling in South-West France*, Viking, Melbourne, 2002.

—— *Stephanie's Journal*, Viking, Melbourne, 1999.

—— *Stephanie's Seasons*, Allen & Unwin, Sydney, 1993.

—— *Stephanie's Australia*, Allen & Unwin, Sydney, 1991.

—— *Stephanie's Feasts and Stories*, Allen & Unwin, Sydney, 1988.

—— *Stephanie's Menus for Food Lovers*, Methuen Haynes, Sydney, 1985.

Alexander, Stephanie and Beer, Maggie, *Stephanie Alexander & Maggie Beer's Tuscan Cookbook*, Viking, Melbourne, 1998.

Anderson, Ronald, *Gold on Four Feet*, Ronald Anderson, Melbourne, 1978.

Andrews, Colman, *Catalan Cuisine*, Headline, London, 1989.

The Barossa Cookery Book, Soldiers' Memorial Institute, Tanunda, 1917.

Beck, Simone, *Simca's Cuisine*, Vintage Books, New York, 1976.

Beck, Simone, Bertholle, Louisette and Child, Julia, *Mastering the Art of French Cooking, Volume One*, Penguin, Harmondsworth, 1979.

Beer, Maggie, *Maggie's Table*, Lantern, Melbourne, 2005.

—— *Cooking with Verjuice*, Penguin, Melbourne, 2003.

—— *Maggie's Orchard*, Viking, Melbourne, 1997.

—— *Maggie's Farm*, Allen & Unwin, Sydney, 1993.

Beeton, Mrs, *Mrs Beeton's Book of Household Management*, Cassell, London, 2000.

—— *Family Cookery*, Ward Lock, London, 1963.

Bertolli, Paul with Waters, Alice, *Chez Panisse Cooking*, Random House, New York, 1988.

Bissell, Frances, *A Cook's Calendar: Seasonal Menus by Frances Bissell*, Chatto & Windus, London, 1985.

Boddy, Michael and Boddy, Janet, *Kitchen Talk Magazine* (vol. I, no's 1–13), The Bugle Press, via Binalong, NSW, 1989–92.

Boni, Ada, *Italian Regional Cooking*, Bonanza Books, New York, 1969.

von Bremzen, Anya and Welchman, John, *Please to the Table: The Russian Cookbook*, Workman, New York, 1990.

Bureau of Resource Sciences, *Marketing Names for Fish and Seafood in Australia*, Department of Primary Industries & Energy and the Fisheries Research & Development Corporation, Canberra, 1995.

Carluccio, Antonio, *A Passion for Mushrooms*, Pavilion Books, London, 1989.

—— *An Invitation to Italian Cooking*, Pavilion Books, London, 1986.

Castelvetro, Giacomo, *The Fruit, Herbs and Vegetables of Italy*, Viking, New York, 1990.

Colmagro, Suzanne, Collins, Graham and Sedgley, Margaret, 'Processing Technology of the Table Olive', University of Adelaide, in Jules Janick (ed.) *Horticultural Reviews* Vol. 25, John Wiley & Sons, 2000.

Cox, Nicola, *Game Cookery*, Victor Gollancz, London, 1989.

David, Elizabeth, *Italian Food*, Penguin, Harmondsworth, 1989.

—— *An Omelette and a Glass of Wine*, Penguin, Harmondsworth, 1986.

—— *English Bread and Yeast Cookery*, Penguin, Harmondsworth, 1979.

—— *French Provincial Cooking*, Penguin, Harmondsworth, 1970.

—— *Summer Cooking*, Penguin, Harmondsworth, 1965.

De Groot, Roy Andries, *The Auberge of the Flowering Hearth*, The Ecco Press, New Jersey, 1973.

Dolamore, Anne, *The Essential Olive Oil Companion*, Macmillan, Melbourne, 1988.

Ferguson, Jenny, *Cooking for You and Me*, Methuen Haynes, Sydney, 1987.

Field, Carol, *Celebrating Italy*, William Morrow, New York, 1990.

Fitzgibbon, Theodora, *Game Cooking*, Andre Deutsch, London, 1963.

Glowinski, Louis, *The Complete Book of Fruit Growing in Australia*, Lothian, Melbourne, 1991.

Gray, Patience, *Honey From a Weed*, Prospect Books, London, 1986.

Gray, Rose and Rogers, Ruth, *The River Cafe Cook Book*, Ebury Press, London, 1996.

Grigson, Jane and Fullick, Roy (eds), *The Enjoyment of Food: The Best of Jane Grigson*, Michael Joseph, London, 1992.

Grigson, Jane, *Jane Grigson's Fruit Book*, Michael Joseph, London, 1982.

—— *Jane Grigson's Vegetable Book*, Penguin, Harmondsworth, 1980.

—— *Good Things*, Penguin, Harmondsworth, 1973.

—— *Jane Grigson's Fish Book*, Penguin, Harmondsworth, 1973.

—— *Charcuterie and French Pork Cookery*, Penguin, Harmondsworth, 1970.

Halligan, Marion, *Eat My Words*, Angus & Robertson, Sydney, 1990.

Hazan, Marcella, *The Classic Italian Cookbook*, Macmillan, London (rev. ed.), 1987.

Hopkinson, Simon with Bareham, Lindsey, *Roast Chicken and Other Stories*, Ebury Press, London, 1994.

Huxley, Aldous, *The Olive Tree*, Ayer, USA, reprint of 1937 ed.

Isaacs, Jennifer, *Bush Food*, Weldon, Sydney, 1987.

Kamman, Madeleine, *In Madeleine's Kitchen*, Macmillan, New York, 1992.

—— *The Making of a Cook*, Atheneum, New York, 1978.

Lake, Max, *Scents and Sensuality*, Penguin, Melbourne, 1991.

Manfield, Christine, *Christine Manfield Originals*, Lantern, Melbourne, 2006.

McGee, Harold, *The Curious Cook*, Northpoint Press, San Francisco, 1990.

—— *On Food and Cooking*, Collier Books, New York, 1988.

Ministero Agricoltura e Foreste. D.O.C. *Cheeses of Italy* (trans. Angela Zanotti), Milan, 1992.

Molyneux, Joyce, with Grigson, Sophie, *The Carved Angel Cookery Book*, Collins, 1990.

Newell, Patrice, *The Olive Grove*, Penguin, Melbourne, 2000.

del Nero, Constance and del Nero, Rosario, *Risotto*, Harper and Row, New York, 1989.

Olney, Richard, *Simple French Food*, Atheneum, New York, 1980.

Peck, Paula, *The Art of Fine Baking*, Simon & Schuster, New York, 1961.

Pellegrini, Angelo M., *The Food Lover's Garden*, Lyons & Burford, New York, 1970.

Pepin, Jacques, *La Technique*, Hamlyn Publishing Group, New York, 1978.

Perry, Neil, *The Food I Love*, Murdoch Books, Sydney, 2005.

Pignolet, Damien, *French*, Lantern, Melbourne, 2005.

Reichelt, Karen, with Burr, Michael, *Extra Virgin: An Australian Companion to Olives and Olive Oil*, Wakefield Press, Adelaide, 1997.

Ripe, Cherry, *Goodbye Culinary Cringe*, Allen & Unwin, Sydney, 1993.

Santich, Barbara, 'The Return of Verjuice', *Winestate*, June 1984.

Schauer, Amy, *The Schauer Australian Cookery Book* (14th ed.), W.R. Smith & Paterson, Brisbane, 1979.

Scicolone, Michele, *The Antipasto Table*, Morrow, New York, 1991.

Scott, Philippa, *Gourmet Game*, Simon & Schuster, New York, 1989.

Silverton, Nancy, *Nancy Silverton's Pastries from the La Brea Bakery*, Random House, New York, 2000.

Simeti, Mary Taylor, *Pomp and Sustenance*, Alfred A. Knopf, New York, 1989.

Stobart, Tom (ed.), *The Cook's Encyclopaedia*, Papermac, London, 1982.

Studd, Will, *Chalk and Cheese*, Purple Egg, Melbourne, 2004.

Sutherland Smith, Beverley, *A Taste for All Seasons*, Lansdowne, Sydney, 1975.

Sweeney, Susan, *The Olive Press*, The Australian Olive Association, Autumn 2006.

Symons, Michael, *One Continuous Picnic*, Duck Press, Adelaide, 1982.

Taruschio, Ann and Taruschio, Franco, *Leaves from the Walnut Tree*, Pavilion, London, 1993.

Time-Life Fruit Book, Time-Life, Amsterdam, 1983.

Wark, Alf, *Wine Cookery*, Rigby, Adelaide, 1969.

Waters, Alice, Curtan, Patricia and Labro, Martine, *Chez Panisse Pasta, Pizza and Calzone*, Random House, New York, 1984.

Waters, Alice, *Chez Panisse Café Cookbook*, Random House, New York, 1999.

—— *Chez Panisse Menu Cookbook*, Chatto & Windus, London, 1984.

Weir, Joanne, *You Say Tomato*, Broadway Books, New York, 1998.

Wells, Patricia, *At Home in Provence*, Scribner, New York, 1996.

Wells, Patricia and Robuchon, Joël, *Simply French*, William Morrow, New York, 1991.

Whiteaker, Stafford, *The Compleat Strawberry*, Century Publishing, London, 1985.

Wolfert, Paula, *The Cooking of the Eastern Mediterranean*, Harper Collins Publishers, New York, 1994.

—— *The Cooking of South-West France*, The Dial Press, New York, 1983.

—— *Mediterranean Cooking*, The Ecco Press, New York, 1977.

Zalokar, Sophie, *Picnic*, Fremantle Arts Centre Press, Perth, 2002.

ACKNOWLEDGEMENTS

This extract from *Maggie's Harvest* represents the culmination of a life's work to date, so how can I possibly conjure up all the people who have been instrumental in so many ways over the years?

My husband, Colin, is my rock – a true partner in every sense of the word. My daughters, Saskia and Elli, have grown into strong, independent women and we share regular boisterous meals with their partners and our much-loved grandchildren, Zöe, Max, Lilly, Rory and Ben – and Darby Saskia, who arrived in January 2015 just before my 70th birthday.

The indomitable Julie Gibbs, originally suggested an update of *Maggie's Farm* and *Maggie's Orchard*, an idea which developed over time into *Maggie's Harvest*. I always had faith in Julie's extraordinary ability to know just what will make a book special.

Photographer Mark Chew effortlessly captured the essence of the produce in the book – it feels so Barossan! Daniel New, the book's designer, weaved his magic with the design. Marie Anne Pledger not only helped out on the shoots, but provided paraphernalia from her own kitchen and that of her friends for us to use.

There are so many in the team at Penguin I'd like to thank. My editors Kathleen Gandy and Virginia Birch and Nicole Brown for keeping us all on track, Anouska Jones for proof-reading, and Jocelyn Hungerford and all at Penguin for eleventh-hour assistance.

Over the years I have had an incredible array of staff who have contributed so much to both my business and my life. First and foremost was the lovely Hilda Laurencis, who sadly died as I wrote the very last pages of *Maggie's Harvest*.

From the Pheasant Farm Restaurant days, Sophie Zalokar, Steve Flamsteed, Nat Paull and Alex Herbert remain part of our extended family, and more recently Victoria Blumenstein and Gill Radford have both done much to ease my daily life.

The friendly, hard-working team at the Farmshop are the public face of our business and help to keep the tradition of the farm alive. I have so much to thank them for. Our customers, from the early days of the Pheasant Farm Restaurant, to those who buy our products all over the world today, have believed in us and what we've done.

I would also like to thank the following people who have lent their expertise in specific areas: Louis Glowinski; Rod Mailer of Evoo; Geoff Lintern vinegar; and Richard Gunner of Coorong Angus Beef, for his passionate endeavours and wealth of knowledge on beef and lamb.

INDEX

LANTERN

UK | USA | Canada | Ireland | Australia
India | New Zealand | South Africa | China

Penguin Books is part of the Penguin Random House group of companies whose
addresses can be found at global.penguinrandomhouse.com.

First published by Penguin Group (Australia), 2015
This material was originally published as a section of *Maggie's Harvest* by Maggie Beer

1 3 5 7 9 10 8 6 4 2

Cover and text design by Daniel New © Penguin Group (Australia)
Design coordination by Hannah Schubert
Typeset in Cochin by Post Pre-Press Group, Brisbane, Queensland
Colour reproduction by Splitting Image, Clayton, Victoria
Printed in China by 1010 Printing International Limited

National Library of Australia
Cataloguing-in-Publication data:

Beer, Maggie.
Maggie Beer's Spring Harvest Recipes.
Notes: Includes bibliographical details and index
ISBN 9781921384233 (pbk.)
Subjects: Seasonal cooking
Other Creators/Contributors:
Chew, Mark, photographer.
641.564

penguin.com.au/lantern

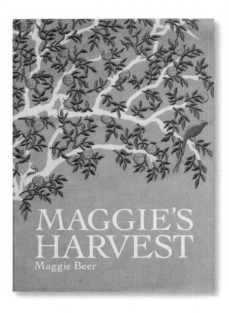

This landmark book from one of Australia's best-loved cooks
was first published in 2007 and will be available
as four seasonal paperbacks.

ISBN: 9781921384240   ISBN: 9781921384257   ISBN: 9781921384226